How to Guide

Keeping Volunteers

A guide to retaining good people

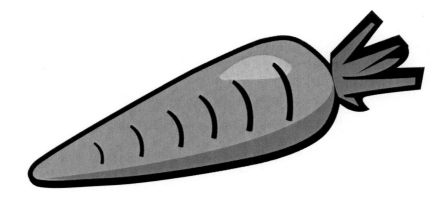

Steve McCurley
Rick Lynch

DIRECTORY OF SOCIAL CHANGE

Published by:

Directory of Social Change
24 Stephenson Way
London NW1 2DP
Tel: 08450 77 77 07, fax: 020 7391 4804
E-mail: publications@dsc.org.uk
Website: www.dsc.org.uk
from whom further copies and a full publications list are available.

The Directory of Social Change is a Registered Charity no. 800517

First published 2007
Reprinted 2010
Copyright © Steve McCurley and Rick Lynch

ISBN 978 1 903991 90 9

British Library Cataloguing in Publication Data
A catalogue record for this book is available from the British Library

Cover design by Tessa Pellow
Designed by Sarah Nicholson
Typeset by Marlinzo Services
Printed by CPI Antony Rowe, Chippenham, Wiltshire

Directory of Social Change London Office:
08450 77 77 07

Directory of Social Change Liverpool Office:
Federation House, Hope Street, Liverpool L1 9BW
0151 708 0136

FSC
www.fsc.org
MIX
Paper from
responsible sources
FSC® C013604

CONTENTS

ABOUT THE AUTHORS

Steve McCurley

Steve McCurley is an internationally-known trainer and speaker in the field of effective volunteer involvement. He is currently a partner in VM Systems, a management consulting firm specialising in helping organisations improve their utilisation of volunteers. In the US Steve has worked with almost every national voluntary organisation, including groups such as the American Association of Retired Persons, Special Olympics International, the Nature Conservancy, the Points of Light Foundation and many others. He has been involved in most of the innovations in volunteering over the past 20 years, including workplace volunteering, online and family volunteering, and the development of the Volunteer Center network.

In the UK Steve has worked with the British Red Cross, Tearfund, VSO, Guide Dogs for the Blind, Community Service Volunteers, Volunteering England and others. On the international front, Steve has done work in Canada, Ireland, the Caribbean, France, Australia, Germany and Brazil.

He is the author of 15 books and more than 150 articles on volunteer involvement and co-author of *Essential Volunteer Management*, published by the Directory of Social Change. His writings have been translated into Spanish, Portuguese, Russian, Romanian, Hebrew, Chinese and Korean, among other languages.

He is the co-editor with Susan Ellis of the *e-Volunteerism* online journal. He is one of the founding faculty of the Institute on Advanced Volunteer Management, held in the UK each year.

Steve can be reached at shm12@aol.com.

Rick Lynch

Richard is a Seattle-based management consultant who specialises in issues relating to not-for-profit organisations. He has done volunteer management workshops in the US, Canada, Australia, Britain, Russia and Singapore. Each year, he speaks at approximately 100 workshops, conventions and conferences in North America and Europe on topics related to volunteer management and leadership effectiveness.

He is the author of the following books:
- *Lead!: How public and non-profit managers can bring out the best in themselves and their organizations.*
- *Getting Out of Your Own Way*
- *Precision Management*

He is also the co-author of *Secrets of Leadership* and *Volunteer Management*, the best-selling book in its field in the US, China and the Ukraine. The British version, *Essential Volunteer Management*, is the best-selling book in its field in the United Kingdom.

Before starting his own firm in 1977, Rick worked for five years as a project director and senior trainer for three management-consulting firms in New York and Washington DC. He holds a masters degree from the University of Iowa.

Rick's experience in the field of volunteer management includes work as a volunteer coordinator and as the training director for the Washington State Office of Voluntary Action, where he set up a unique system of delivering management training to volunteer directors through a network of volunteer training organisers. He has served on the boards of directors of a number of non-profit organisations, including a volunteer centre, a retired senior volunteer programme, a United Way, national and local literacy programmes, and National CASA, an organisation that ensures that abused children are placed in safe and permanent homes. He has been a featured speaker on volunteer management at international, national, international and state conferences since 1979.

At various times during his career, Rick has served as a reading teacher, a bass player in a blues band and chief of a volunteer fire department.

FOREWORD

Retaining volunteers is a critical focus of any effective volunteer programme. Much is written and debated about effective ways to recruit volunteers but, in the final analysis, if they don't stay with you when recruited your efforts have been in vain. Retention is, in some ways, the more important yet poorer cousin to the more glamorous topic of recruitment.

It is perhaps not surprising then that few volunteer management books have been devoted to retaining volunteers. Into this relative void comes this excellent new book from Steve McCurley and Rick Lynch, authors of the acclaimed *Essential Volunteer Management*.

The volume you hold in your hands takes a comprehensive look at retention, journeying from why it is a key issue in volunteer management to how to handle volunteer burnout. On your journey though this book you'll be challenged to think afresh about how to retain volunteers in the 21st century, especially with the advent of shorter-term volunteer assignments; how to make volunteers feel special; how to sustain retention along the volunteer life cycle and how to create meaningful roles for volunteers.

Keeping Volunteers has much to offer the field of volunteer management, whether in voluntary, community, public or private sector. Written in a straightforward way, it is practical, challenging and informative, whether you are new to the role of volunteer manager or a practitioner of long standing.

Steve McCurley and Rick Lynch have, once again, given the field what will become a standard text on a critical but oft-overlooked area of volunteerism.

Rob Jackson
Director of Volunteering Development and Grant Making
Volunteering England

THE EMERGING ISSUE OF RETAINING VOLUNTEERS

Most organisations seeking to involve volunteers focus on the act of recruitment. Programme managers worry about having enough volunteers, constantly engage in efforts to attract new volunteers and generally spend much time and effort attempting to replace volunteers they have lost.

Viewed rationally, this approach is costly and cumbersome. Recruiting new volunteers can be time-consuming and expensive. Interviewing and screening volunteers entails both financial and staff resources. Training volunteers – especially for more skilled volunteer positions – can be extremely expensive. Hollway (2002) reports that the average cost of recruiting and training a new volunteer at the 2000 Olympic Games in Sydney was AUD $700. And then, of course, there are the negative costs associated with poor volunteer retention – the loss of skilled workers and the possibility of bad community relations as disgruntled volunteers share their opinions with others. Fischer and Shaffer (1993) commented:

> ... volunteers who quit after a short time are costly. Typically, ex-volunteers or almost-volunteers take away their acquired learning and leave little behind ... Turnover, especially high turnover, can create havoc in the administration and management of volunteer programs. A vicious cycle may be set up: there may be no point in training or spending time with volunteers if most of them are going to quit shortly anyway. However, if volunteers are given no training or guidance, the quality of their work is not likely to be good. If their work is not good, they will feel incompetent and frustrated, and soon they will quit.

While the loss of volunteers is detrimental to all organisations, for some programmes it can have a devastating effect. Grossman and Furano (2002) noted the consequences of loss of volunteers whose role is forming relationships with some types of clients:

> Selecting a volunteer who can honor his time commitment is particularly important when the volunteer's job, whether primarily or secondarily, is to

form a relationship with others. Vulnerable individuals, such as the youth or the elderly, can be emotionally damaged when good-hearted volunteers who start befriending decide they really do not have the time to continue. Feelings of rejection and disappointment, on the part of the children in particular, may lead to a host of negative emotional, behavioral, and academic outcomes.

Loss of volunteers can also affect charitable organisations in other ways. Zappala and Burrell (2002) noted the relationship between volunteering and contributing money at The Smith Family (TSF), a large charity in Australia:

> Our findings suggest that those volunteers that have been associated with TSF for longer periods of time were significantly more likely to make larger financial contributions compared to those that were relatively new to the organisation. Having loyal volunteers pays in more ways than one! The loss of long-serving volunteers may therefore have fundraising as well as human resource implications. Once again, this suggests that there are broader gains for nonprofit organisations in adopting a strategic approach to volunteer management. The costs of volunteer turnover, for instance, may be greater than those traditionally associated with employee turnover for organisations that rely on volunteers and for whom fundraising is a significant proportion of their income. At the very least, these findings suggest that fundraising and volunteer management personnel within nonprofit organisations have much to gain by working more closely together.

According to Penner (2002) '... it can be argued that if service organizations face a personnel problem, it is not a shortage of people who want to volunteer. Instead, it is an attrition among people in the early stages of their tenure with the organization.'

This simple point led the National Health and Medical Research Council of Australia to comment in 2003:

> Maintenance of a stable, long-term volunteer workforce should be a major goal of volunteer management to save time in recruiting and training and to retain the confidence of paid staff in the volunteers.

It is far better to focus on maintaining those volunteers who are already involved with the programme, avoiding the expense of interviewing and training new volunteers, and the productivity lost when inexperienced volunteers have to learn how best to approach their work.

Rising concern about retention

Volunteer retention is an area of increasing concern to voluntary organisations. In the Local Voluntary Action Surveys conducted by the Home Office in 1999, the majority of voluntary organisations in local UK communities reported increased difficulties with retention of volunteers, an indication of the growing difficulty some charities are having in maintaining their volunteer force. A 2001 study of fire brigade volunteers in New Zealand (UMR Research) found that 'More than half of all volunteers from composite brigades surveyed said they are concerned about volunteer turnover, and 41% of rural volunteers surveyed said they are concerned about turnover in their force.' Daly (1991) reported that high turnover of volunteers had become a problem for 56% of sporting organisations.

A 2003 Canadian survey of volunteer managers by Environics Research Group ranked 'retention' third in the challenges faced in programme management. Cuskelly and Boag (2001) reported that volunteer turnover is a problem for 56% of Australian sport organisations. A 2003 report on volunteering in sports programmes in the UK (Leisure Industries Research Centre) noted that: 'retaining volunteers is increasingly difficult, and currently there is one "lapsed" volunteer for every two active volunteers.' Elstad (2003), in a study of volunteers for a jazz festival in Norway, discovered that 30% of them had considered leaving.

A 2003 study of volunteers in social service agencies in Toronto (Toronto Community and Neighborhood Services 2004) found that 'Fifty-three percent of responding agencies said they were successful in retaining their volunteers. Forty percent said they were successful some of the time and seven per cent said they could not keep volunteers.' A 2004 report by Statistics Canada noted that 49% of organisations reported 'difficulty in retaining volunteers' as a problem.

Handy et al, in a 2004 examination of volunteers in Canadian hospitals, reported that the number of volunteers who remained involved for five years or longer had decreased at 80% of hospital sites.

Organisations are slowly beginning to realise that operating a revolving door volunteer programme is highly ineffective.

Why volunteers discontinue volunteering

Volunteers choose to stop volunteering for a number of reasons. Some of these reasons are beyond the control of an organisation or of the volunteer. Others are not. A study in the United States undertaken by the United Parcel Service

Foundation (1998) discovered that after 'conflicts with more pressing demands' (65%), poor volunteer management was the most frequent reason cited to explain why people stop volunteering:

	%
● Charity was not well managed	26
● Charity did not use volunteers' time well	23
● Charity did not use volunteers' talents well	18
● Volunteers' tasks were not clearly defined	16
● Volunteers were not thanked	9

Their conclusion was straightforward:

> Poor volunteer management practices result in more lost volunteers than people losing interest because of changing personal or family needs. The best way for volunteer organizations to receive more hours of volunteer service is to be careful managers of the time already being volunteered by people of all ages and from all strata of our volunteer society.

Although not having enough time is the usual answer that volunteers will give for leaving a programme, we suspect that this is often an excuse. When people really want to do something in their lives, they make the time.

A 2002 study of volunteers in Singapore (National Volunteer and Philanthropy Centre) found the following reasons for discontinuing volunteering:

	%
● Too much responsibility	18
● Feeling burnt out	18
● Lack of advancement	17
● Feeling unappreciated	16

Princeton Survey Research Associates in a 1998 study of young US volunteers found that 'feeling that the group was disorganized or its expectations were unclear (24%) and that they themselves did not respect their supervisors or co-workers (19%) are the chief reasons given by young people who report having a bad experience with a community-based organization.'

Raskoff and Sundeen (1999) in a study of high school community service projects in Los Angeles found that students:

> ... disliked being bored, not making a difference, not feeling appreciated or recognized, being required to serve, not receiving pay for their work, sensing a lack of commitment by others towards volunteerism, having to do too

much work, and doing specific types of work, such as cleaning up. Also, people who were annoying and the presence of people in need or suffering were a concern for some students.

In all, 80% of students reported at least one source of dissatisfaction.

Turnoffs to volunteering reported by 45 volunteers interviewed in Ottawa in 1992 (Ancans) included:

- disorganised management
- lack of board support
- staff indifference
- limited training and orientation
- lack of contact and support
- wrong assignment
- perks that are withdrawn
- insufficient funding.

In Australia, the Australian Bureau of Statistics (1995) found the following sources of dissatisfaction among volunteers:

	%
• Relationships with paid staff	2.1
• Amount/adequacy of supervision	2.4
• Amount/adequacy of training	4.9
• Lack of recognition	5.7
• Insurance cover	5.9
• Risk of injury/health	6.1
• Costs	6.7
• Travel/distance/location	7.3
• Amount of time required	10.4
• Legal responsibility	10.5
• Lack of support	11.6
• No concerns	64.2

DeMarco (1998) found that '24% of Ontarians indicate that a major obstacle to volunteering is that volunteers are not treated well.' Lasby (2004) reported that eight per cent of Canadians indicated that a previous bad volunteer experience kept them from volunteering further. Guseh and Winders (2002) found in a North Carolina study of volunteerism that:

Bad experiences in the past discouraged 15 percent of non-volunteers from contributing any time, and 26 percent of volunteers would have contributed more time had they not been frustrated by such experiences.

The 1997 National Survey of Volunteering in the UK (Institute for Volunteering Research, 1997) uncovered similar responses. Here are the percentages of volunteers reporting on their perceptions of the drawbacks of volunteering:

	%
● Things could be better organised	71
● You sometimes get bored or lose interest	34
● You can't always cope with the things you are asked to do	30
● You don't get asked to do the things you'd like to do	20
● It takes up too much time	31
● Your help is not really wanted	5
● Your efforts aren't always appreciated	29
● Too much is expected of you	20
● The organisation isn't really going anywhere	16
● You find yourself out of pocket	29

Many of these reasons, you will note, hinge upon the type of working relationship established between the volunteer and the organisation – whether that relationship is meaningful, rewarding and productive. They are, accordingly, contingent upon the presence or absence of effective volunteer management. Organisations that work effectively at keeping volunteers are less likely to experience difficulties in retention.

The difficulty of measuring effective retention

Very little useful information exists on volunteer retention rates, especially if one is attempting to identify a numerical goal or standard that might be applicable to one's own volunteer programme. Fischer and Shaffer (1993), in studying programmes that involved older volunteers, found that only 30% of programmes gathered data on the numbers of volunteers who left the programme and most of this data was very limited in scope. It is difficult, therefore, to recommend a percentage or time goal that might be used as a standard for measuring the appropriateness or effectiveness of retention techniques. This is true for a number of reasons:

1. Volunteers move in to and out of volunteering

Studies of volunteer participation over time indicate that volunteers typically go through periods of volunteering and not volunteering. Segal (1993), for example, found that, while 20% of women in a US National Longitudinal Study were volunteering at any given time, only about nine per cent volunteered throughout the 15-year term of the study. Johnson et al (2004), in a study of US women's volunteer participation from 1940 to 1960, found that individuals moved in to and out of community service over time, with patterns of participation showing a great deal of variability.

Feeney (2001) noted in a study of volunteer involvement in New Zealand that:

> Volunteering with different organizations at different times of their lives depending on their interests and family commitments was seen to be a general pattern. People often started volunteering by becoming involved with their children's activities then moving to more formal roles within those organizations. Volunteers might work for several organizations at the same time but usually with varying levels of commitment.

Intermittent involvement is probably the normal pattern for volunteering, with relatively few volunteers being involved at all points of their lives, much less being involved with the same organisation over that entire time.

Some organisations have begun to recognise that they may have different groups of volunteers who will tend to stay with the organisation for different periods. The US American Red Cross, for example, groups volunteers into the following operational categories:

Registered volunteers

Registered volunteers are those who have demonstrated an ongoing commitment to the Red Cross and whose names and addresses are on file at the chapter (branch) or station.

Registered for credit volunteers

Registered for credit volunteers receive a formalised *quid pro quo* (a reciprocal exchange) from the Red Cross. Registered for credit volunteers include students performing service learning, court-mandated community service participants, interns and others.

Unregistered volunteers

Unregistered volunteers are those who participate only briefly for a single time or a special event, for whom no paperwork is completed.

An organisation may expect the second two categories to have different retention rates from those who have made an ongoing commitment, although as is shown in Chapter 10, one of the key aspects of retention in years to come will be convincing these short-term volunteers to move to a longer relationship.

2. Programmes may have very different retention rates

Black and Kovacs (1999) noted the results of some studies of volunteer retention rates in hospice programmes in the United States:

> Studies focusing on hospice programs have reported varying retention rates of volunteers. Amenta (1984) found that 43% of volunteers left a hospice program between 4 and 11 months after completing training, whereas Finn Paradis and Usui (1987) found that 28% of the volunteers left 4 months after completing training. Black and Kovacs's (1996) study of hospice programs found that volunteers had served an average of 4.75 years, and approximately 80% of the volunteers predicted that they would continue serving for more than 2 years.

A 1997 study of volunteers by Community Literacy of Ontario determined that the average volunteer tenure of literacy volunteers was 3.71 years, but with 26% of volunteers having initiated volunteering within the past year, 45% having joined the agency within the past two years, and 30% having volunteered for over five years. Griffiths (2003), in a study of meals on wheels volunteers in New South Wales, found that 37% had been volunteering for more than 10 years and 26.1% for between five and ten years. Balliette and Smith (1990), in a study of 4-H volunteer leaders in Nevada (4-H is a North American youth club which encourages learning and leadership) found that 'the turnover among adult volunteers in the local 4-H programme averaged 42% a year from 1981–1988.' Taylor et al (2003) reported that among chairs and secretaries in sports clubs in England 60% had been involved for more than 10 years. Breaux (1993) found that the average duration of volunteers in active service in an AIDS programme in Houston was 643 days.

A study of Extension volunteers (a US volunteer programme serving those in rural communities through educational and agricultural assistance programmes), (Steele, 1986) found the following pattern:

Age	%
• 0–1	7
• 2–4	25
• 5–9	25
• 10–19	26
• 20+	17

A 2001 survey of Court Appointed Special Advocate (CASA) programmes in the United States discovered an average volunteer length of service of 2.6 years, but CASA is by far one of the most intensive and difficult volunteer positions, so turnover is not unlikely. CASA is also, on the other hand, typically one of the better managed volunteer programmes in a community; a factor likely to improve volunteer commitment.

Similarly, Nelson et al (2004a) found that the Oregon long-term care ombudsman programme had had an average turnover rate of 22% annually since 1981, but noted: 'Given the difficulty of the ombudsman's job, this rate does not, on the face of it, seem unduly onerous.'

Lysakowski (2003) found the following pattern of volunteer longevity among fundraising volunteers in the US:

	%
• less than one year	14
• one to two years	17
• three to five years	25
• six to nine years	9
• more than nine years	7

Musgrove (2001) reported on a new volunteer project at the homelessness charity, St Mungo's, in London, in which over a three-year period 1,300 potential volunteers stepped forward – only to result in a volunteer base of just 50. Is this a failure in retention or just the reality of a volunteer programme in which the degree of volunteer commitment required is much higher than that of others?

Fahey and Walker (2001) reported that among volunteer ambulance officers in Tasmania:

> The average length of time respondents had been members was 4.5 years with a minimum of 0.2 and a maximum of 39 years. All together 16% of respondents had been members for less than one year, 43% for 1–5 years, 30% for 5–10 years and 9% for over 10 years.

But they went on to note that '... there is a high turnover of recruits within the first few months and suggested figures of 30–50% within the first year.'

In one of the larger general US studies, Hager and Brudney (2004) asked those responsible for volunteer management in organisations 'of the volunteers that worked with your organisation one year ago, approximately what percentage would you say are still involved as volunteers?' The median rate was 80%, with 17% reporting 100% retention and three per cent reporting nil retention. The

Australian Bureau of Statistics in a 2001 study reported '40% of volunteers had been working for their current types of organisations for at least six years and around 25% for more than 10 years.'

We simply do not have enough data to identify appropriate percentages, especially given the wide variation in programmes – time available, degree of management support, type of volunteers involved and so on.

Many programmes have difficulty even beginning to track retention rates since they may have volunteers who are 'enrolled' but who have not volunteered recently and thus it is unclear whether they are still available for service or have left the organisation. If you have no specific term of commitment and volunteers can easily move in to and out of participation, how do you measure attrition? Heritage Link (2003), in a study of volunteers in historic environment organisations in the UK, noted that while the two largest (The National Trust and English Heritage) had almost 445,000 members, only about 6.5% were 'active participants'.

Almost every new volunteer programme manager encounters a roster of far more volunteers than are actually volunteering at that time. Some of these turn out to be phantoms.

3. High retention rates are not always a good thing

While, in general, high rates of volunteer retention are good, there are exceptions to this rule.

If your volunteer programme focuses on recruiting short-term volunteers for projects, then you are likely to see high levels of turnover amongst these volunteers. Zappala et al (2001) suggested that in the 'social enterprise' model of volunteering, in which young people and corporate employees are recruited for fixed-term one-off projects, 'regularity of service is not required.' In addition, some categories of volunteers – students and young people, for example – will tend towards shorter volunteer engagements, especially if their motivation for volunteering was connected to gaining work experience or if they are near to relocating.

In addition, turnover among volunteer programmes can be productive if it is connected to bringing 'new blood' into the volunteer pool.

Organisations that rely on the same volunteers over extended periods tend to produce a 'cloning' effect, ending up with volunteers who are extremely similar. This in turn makes recruiting more difficult as it becomes immediately obvious to newcomers that they may not 'fit' the volunteer pattern.

The best example of this phenomenon in the United States is that of hospital auxiliary volunteer programmes (McCurley, 1999, 2001) that have a demographic profile – female, above the age of 70, Caucasian, middle-class – which is both incredibly narrow and quite different from the common range of volunteers; a profile that developed over time due to the lack of need to involve new volunteers because of the extremely high retention rates of existing volunteers.

In Griffiths' (2003) study of meals on wheels volunteers in New South Wales she found that the lowest percentage of volunteers were those who had been volunteering for less than a year (8.7%), suggesting that they may also follow this pattern of slow decline. Fraser and Gottlieb (2001) have examined this same phenomenon of ageing and slow decline among long-term care volunteers in Canada.

Aldridge, in a study of emergency fire and rescue services in Queensland, Australia (2003), noted: 'An interesting statistic provided by the QFRS [Queensland Fire and Rescue Service] was that in 1950 the average volunteer starting age was 18. In 2001 it had risen to an average starting age of 31.' Over 80% of the fire and rescue services in his study reported that they would have a problem with an ageing volunteer population in the not-too-distant future.

Many arts and culture volunteer programmes are facing a similar situation. The Canadian Museums Association in a 2001 report noted impending problems due to an ageing volunteer population:

> Canada experienced a major expansion of museums through the late 60s and 70s, an expansion often inspired and led by volunteers. A cyclical 'bulge' in attrition aggravates the current trend as many founding volunteers simply retire with advancing age.

Determining whether your volunteer programme suffers from poor retention is necessarily, then, a matter of closely examining what is happening. This requires keeping records of when and why volunteers choose to leave the organisation and seeing if negative patterns develop. It is difficult to resolve a retention problem when you have no idea why it is occurring.

Another approach is to survey volunteers periodically in order to determine their levels of satisfaction and dissatisfaction or to determine factors that might lead to the departure of a volunteer. McMurray (1993), for example, in a study of early match closures among Big Brother volunteers (an international volunteer agency that mentors children) in Ontario found:

Also, most Big Brothers said their matches fell short of their expectations and felt their relationships ended up being more of a 'struggle' then they had anticipated. Some of the more common suggestions from volunteers for agencies to reduce the rate of early match closures included: utilizing more scenarios or situational questions during orientation; informing new Big Brothers of the 'realities' of volunteering (that is, potential problems, work involved); encouraging more interaction between new and experienced Big Brothers; and maintaining more contact and support of volunteers within the first year of the match. The interviews suggested that matches ending within the first year were related to either the volunteer's expectations not being met or the difficulties that developed from unexpected situations arising during the match.

If nothing else this may give you a quick assessment of the general state of volunteer opinions. Bell (2003), for example, in a study of volunteers with the Department of Conservation (DOC) in New Zealand reported that:

> The majority of respondents either strongly agreed or were inclined to agree that volunteering for DOC is: enjoyable, useful to conservation and satisfying. (Approximately 82% either strongly agreed or were inclined to agree with the statement that volunteering is enjoyable, 83% think it is useful to conservation, and 80% think it is satisfying.) Considerably fewer volunteers agreed or strongly agreed that volunteering is educational or well organized: 33% strongly agreed it is educational and 32% strongly agreed it is well organized.

This can be done either in a formal survey or during evaluative discussions with volunteers. Exit interviews with departing volunteers can be especially instructive. Interviews with those who are considering volunteering can be equally instructive.

The volunteer's side of retention

From the perspective of a volunteer, leaving the organisation may be a perfectly rational notion, especially if they are having a bad experience. The interesting fact is that as we have persuaded more people to volunteer and have given them more experiences with both good and bad volunteer management practices, we have bred a more sophisticated volunteer – one who knows the difference between being managed well and being managed poorly, and one who also knows that if they leave this volunteer position there is another one waiting round the corner.

As Noble et al (2003) put it:

> Volunteers will walk away from organisations failing to provide them with satisfying experiences. Many are highly educated and well informed, and bring with them a great deal of experience to their volunteer position. They expect to be provided with facilities, support, and, where appropriate, training to perform the job. They are not looking to be either ignored or over-regulated. They require and expect that their ideas, skills and experience will be maximised, and to be part of the planning and decision-making processes in a well managed and supportive environment.

As Brudney (1990) noted, this is as true for volunteer programmes in government as it is for charities:

> Government organizations that make a sincere effort to develop a climate receptive to volunteering, match volunteer competencies and preferences to nonpaid positions, adapt the workplace to citizens, and implement outreach policies are more apt to make mutually satisfying volunteer placements that will endure over time.

Michael (1990), in a study of school volunteer programmes sponsored by the National Research Council, summed up this concept as follows: 'Successful programs give much time and attention to the way volunteers are treated.'

Our favourite pithy description of the dangers of not paying sufficient attention to volunteers is provided by Thinktank Research Consultancy (1997), following a study of sports volunteers in Hong Kong: 'Bad feelings with organisations served also caused a stampede for volunteers.'

Nobody volunteers in order to be treated badly.

Our approach to retention

This book focuses on the art of keeping volunteers productively connected to the organisation. 'Retention,' as defined by Jamison (2003) is 'the ability to keep volunteers involved.'

We are going to examine this subject in a variety of ways since, like any aspect of human motivation, volunteer retention is a complex subject that may be approached, and accomplished, through many different means.

We will begin with a quick review of the basis for volunteer retention, examining some of the obvious, but key, points behind what motivates volunteers to become and stay involved.

We will go on to take a deeper look at the psychological factors that create a sense of fulfilment in a volunteer, examining in turn:

- What makes volunteers feel involved in the organisational team rather than feeling like unwanted outsiders?
- What elements in volunteer positions create a meaningful and empowering work experience for volunteers?
- How volunteers can become true believers in the values and cause of an organisation, thus internalising its mission and their own commitment to it – volunteering effectively because it has become 'the right thing to do.'
- How volunteers can be made to feel valued and respected by the organisation in which they work.

These chapters should be viewed as a connected set of factors that together build volunteer retention. They relate to a pattern uncovered by, among others, Chevrier, Steuer and MacKenzie (1994), who found in a survey of US hospice volunteers that volunteer satisfaction was related to feeling like a team member, receiving feedback from staff, feeling valuable and having one's volunteer expectations match their position. We will examine how to create all these feelings and others that relate to retention.

We will then look at volunteer retention from two very different perspectives:

- How an organisation's volunteer involvement processes may either support or deter commitment.
- How the motivational needs of a volunteer are likely to change throughout their relationship with the organisation.

Then we will examine in more depth two special topical areas related to retention:

- Coping with burnout among volunteers.
- Turning short-term volunteers into continuous, long-term volunteers.

And finally, and perhaps somewhat surprisingly in a book on keeping volunteers, we will discuss effective ways of not retaining a volunteer but deliberately releasing them from their relationship with the organisation. In this final chapter we will examine what steps to take when the relationship with the volunteer has failed and the appropriate management response is not to retain the volunteer.

UNDERSTANDING THE BASICS OF VOLUNTEER RETENTION

Volunteers are a precious resource. Without them, charities cannot begin to address their missions effectively. The problems faced by non-profit organisations today are too large to be addressed adequately by paid staff alone. To make an impact, charities must involve significant numbers of volunteers in all aspects of their work.

As a consequence, charities should try to keep volunteers involved as long as possible. Where volunteer turnover is high, there are severe demands on the programme manager to keep recruiting and training new people. Although many volunteers today are often willing to make only a short time commitment to an agency, a significant number of these people can be turned into long-term volunteers through proper retention strategies.

Retaining volunteers is the most important task of the volunteer programme manager in a charity. By keeping the volunteers you have, you will develop a wealth of experience and save vast amounts of time on recruiting, screening and training new volunteers.

At the end of that period, or shortly thereafter, we might persuade the volunteer to make another commitment, perhaps for a longer period. This is made much easier, of course, if the volunteer has had a satisfying volunteer experience and if you have provided them with the means for making progressively larger commitments, a retention concept covered in Chapter 10.

The motivational payback for volunteering

Charities are fuelled by the motivation of their volunteers and staff. Problems of volunteer retention can usually be traced to problems of motivation.

A motivated volunteer is one who wants to do the work that needs to be done in the spirit and within the guidelines of the organisation.

People behave in positive ways when the work satisfies a need they have. Children, for example, are motivated to open birthday presents because doing so meets a psychological need. Starting here, we correctly see that volunteer motivation comes from inside the volunteer, stemming from a set of needs that is satisfied by doing things that are found to be productive.

Sometimes this relationship will be obvious. Smith (2003), for example, discovered that volunteers at literary heritage sites in the UK tended to be motivated through an affinity with the works of the literary figure honoured at the site. Galley and Clifton (2004) found that volunteers at an ecotourism project in Indonesia were eco-centric, a not-surprising conclusion. In other situations determining precise motivations may be more complicated.

When you encounter volunteers whose behaviour is not as you would like, you may label them 'unmotivated', but actually this is incorrect. So-called unmotivated people are actually just as motivated as those who are. Their behaviour meets their motivational needs. However, as this chapter shows, those needs are met in counterproductive ways. They behave in the way they do because that is more satisfying for them than behaving as you would like them to. In other words, people behave the way they do for a particular reason. From the volunteer's perspective their behaviour is always 'rational' because it meets their motivational needs, although it does not necessarily meet yours.

In engaging the interests of volunteers, charities, either formally or informally, enter into what Farmer and Fedor (2003) refer to as a 'psychological contract', a tacit agreement that volunteering will allow the volunteer to meet some of their motivational needs and that the organisation will attempt to facilitate this process.

Paid staff who are unfamiliar with volunteers may be somewhat nervous about this 'motivational' payback, feeling that it gives them less ability to influence or control the work effort of a volunteer than they could that of a paid worker.

In truth, however, 'motivational' paybacks can actually be more powerful than financial ones. Frey and Goette (1999), in one of the most intriguing studies ever done about volunteer motivation, examined the consequences in Switzerland of a procedural change in the treatment accorded volunteers in local political settings. Some of the 'volunteers' were given small financial rewards. After a comparison of the work efforts between these 'paid' volunteers and those who were not receiving any financial rewards, they concluded:

> We find that the incidence of rewards reduces volunteering. While the size of the rewards induces individuals to provide more volunteer work, the mere fact that they receive a payment significantly reduces their work efforts by approximately four hours. The magnitude of these effects is considerable.

Evaluated at the median reward level, volunteers work indeed less ... Direct incentives may backfire, leading to less volunteering.

Money, while it is a powerful motivational force, is not the only motivator, nor is it always the most powerful.

All behaviour is motivated

So-called 'unmotivated' behaviour is caused by frustration of a motivational need. If volunteers have a high need for achievement, for example, and see little to accomplish or 'win' in the assignment, they may set up a win or lose situation with those in authority. A volunteer, for example, might go to the board of directors every time there is a disagreement with the supervisor's decision, seeking to have the decision overturned. This so-called 'unmotivated' behaviour meets the volunteer's need for achievement. It provides a challenge and creates an opportunity to win.

When we talk about motivating volunteers, we are talking about creating a volunteer experience that allows individuals to meet their motivational needs in ways that are productive for the organisation and satisfying for the individual. You remove barriers to motivation by designing satisfying work experiences and creating systems that allow volunteers to meet their needs. You make sure, in other words, that volunteers receive their motivational payback for the valuable contributions they make to the organisation's work. This is the essence of volunteer retention.

Because each volunteer has a different combination of needs, each will do best in different working conditions. Some volunteers may be highly motivated by gaining work experience, whereas others may be highly motivated by the desire to meet new people. Still others may have a burning passion to do something to contribute to the cause. For the first type, you need to make sure that they have the opportunity to learn the skills they want to learn. The second type must be placed in a work setting where they can work with others. The third type needs a position that makes a meaningful contribution to the organisation's mission.

At its most fundamental level, retaining volunteers is a matter of making sure that the volunteer gets what we call 'the motivational payback'. The motivational payback means that the motives that caused the volunteer to come to us in the first place are satisfied by the volunteer experience.

Gaskin (2003) commented: 'Volunteers want to feel welcome, secure, accepted, respected, informed, well-used, and well-managed. Since they do not have "their reward through their pay packet", rewards must be supplied in other ways by the organization.'

People volunteer for a variety of legitimate reasons. Some common ones are:

- to get out of the house or escape boredom
- to meet new people or make new friends
- to gain work experience to help towards finding a new job
- to try out a new career
- to help solve a community problem
- to give something back
- to assuage guilt
- to gain recognition
- to impress an employer
- to make contacts among community leaders
- to gain prestige
- to be in charge of something
- to feel useful
- to learn something new
- to build self-esteem
- to do something different
- to rebuild an old skill
- to help someone else
- to be with friends who volunteer
- to be part of a prestigious group
- to spend 'quality time' with their family by volunteering together
- to make a transition to a new life
- to gain respect
- to meet potential employers
- to make business contacts
- to learn about a community problem
- to gain status
- to express a religious belief or fulfil a moral duty
- to have fun.

Each of these motivations, or combinations of these motivations, can form the basis of motivational payback. People who volunteer because of a desire to make new friends, for example, will experience motivational payback if in fact they do make new friends as part of the volunteer experience. They will not be 'paid' if they are given assignments in which they work alone.

This means that each volunteer needs to be paid in a different motivational currency. The volunteer programme manager needs to ascertain, usually in the interview process, the type of motivational need or combination of needs that caused each volunteer to come forward and then make sure that the volunteer experience satisfies that motivational need.

When we look at the list of common motivators, we can divide them into two categories: motivations that are altruistic (to help others or to solve a community problem) and those that are selfish (to escape boredom or develop a skill). Some assume that the altruistic motivations are more 'valid'. However, we believe that all the motivations are legitimate reasons to volunteer. A study done internally by the Australian charity The Smith Family of its volunteers, found that those volunteering for selfish reasons stayed for longer than those volunteering for altruistic reasons. One reason for this may be that it is harder for volunteers to see the motivational payback if they are volunteering for altruistic reasons.

This is made more complicated by the fact that volunteers usually volunteer for a combination of reasons. Developing work situations that match that combination of reasons is a major challenge to the volunteer programme manager. A person who wants to develop particular work skills and also make a contribution to a cause, for example, requires a position in which those work skills can be developed (and documented for future employers) and in which the work clearly advances a cause.

This is made even more complicated by the fact that the motivational needs of the volunteer may change over time. What attracts people to a charity initially may not motivate them after they have been there for a while. Stewart and Weinstein (1997) noted in a study of AIDS volunteers

> Respondents also provided information about their reasons for continuing participation at the settings. These reasons differed from those for initiating involvement in that continuing motivations were more related to effects and benefits of their work and to the nature of the setting's structure.

Lammers (1991) noted the difference between what he calls the 'predictors of volunteering itself' and the 'predictors of duration'.

Some interesting work has been done in attempting to examine volunteer motivations and match them to volunteer satisfaction, commitment and retention. Clary and Snyder (1991, 1999) and Clary et al (1998) pioneered the use of the Volunteer Functions Inventory (VFI). This groups motivations into the following categories:

- Values ('I feel it is important to help others.')
- Understanding ('Volunteering lets me learn through direct, hands-on experience.')
- Enhancement ('Volunteering makes me feel better about myself.')
- Career ('Volunteering can help me get my foot in the door at a place where I would like to work.')

- Social ('People I know share an interest in community service.')
- Protective ('Volunteering is a good escape from my own troubles.')

They relate these motivations to both recruitment and retention (Clary and Snyder, 1999):

> The importance of matching an individual's motivations to the volunteering situation does not end with recruitment. As participation is an ongoing and sustained activity, functionalist theorizing suggests that volunteers whose motivational concerns are served by their participation would derive greater satisfaction than those whose concerns are not met.

A number of researchers (see, for example, Zappala and Burrell, 2001; Clary et al, 1992; Esmond and Dunlop, 2004) have begun the tedious process of studying various groups of volunteers to determine how differences in initial motivation relate to their further volunteer experience and attitudes.

The basic rules of retention

In this book we are going to cover some sophisticated strategies for retaining volunteers. However, first we will point out some very basic, perhaps obvious, principles that all charity staff should keep in mind. Like many obvious principles, these are often overlooked.

Retention does not happen in a vacuum

Volunteer involvement depends upon the creation of an effective system for working with volunteers. A programme that has insufficient infrastructure, inadequate staff and leadership support, insufficient budgeting or other defects in management will struggle to attract and keep volunteers. Brudney and Gazley (2002) suggested:

> Extensive academic and professional literature supports the rather obvious argument that successful volunteer programs require more than a call for warm bodies. Volunteer programs also require an infrastructure and a set of management tools in order to place the right volunteers in the right positions, involve them effectively and retain them.

Weston et al (2003), for example, found that volunteers with the Australian Threatened Bird Network preferred projects where organisers set clear goals, provided feedback and supervised in a friendly and helpful manner; all basic elements of competent management.

Often the most fundamental manifestation of this support is the presence of a designated member of staff who focuses on making volunteering happen and creating the organisational system to utilise volunteer resources effectively.

Phibbs (2003), in a study in Australia, found that 59% of volunteer-involving organisations did not have a manager or coordinator for their volunteer programme and of those that did only 50% had provided any training for that person.

A 2004 study (CIS Research Centre) of organisations in Alberta, Canada, found that just over half (50.7%) felt that the person in charge of managing their volunteers had the skills and knowledge to perform the job effectively.

Taylor (2003) reported about sports clubs in England that:

> Only 12% of national governing bodies in sports had a volunteer strategy; among individual clubs, only 1% claimed to have a volunteer strategy; 5% of universities, 0% of schools, young persons organisations or disability organisations. 3% of sports clubs had a volunteer coordinator.

LeRoy and Clemens (2003) reported on the results of an assessment of organisations in Canada across various management categories. The category for 'Volunteers included examination of such factors as ratio of volunteer hours to staff hours, recruiting activities, management and development of volunteer resources, donations (other than time) and turnover.' Categories were given scores of 1–10, with 10 being a high rating. The results are depressing:

> The average and median scores for all service categories for Volunteers ... are low, ranging from 4.5 to 6.1. A very small number of agencies scored 8 or above. All service categories contain agencies scoring below 5, which also indicates that there is room for improvement. Nearly one quarter of all agencies, in aggregate, scored below 4, indicating that the need for improvement is widespread. All categories except the Provision of Basic Necessities category had agencies scoring less than 2, which indicates poor performance.

What makes this even more depressing is that it is not a random sample of agencies – it is, instead, an evaluation of agencies that had nominated themselves for the Donner Canadian Foundation Awards for Excellence in the Delivery of Social Services.

A US report (Urban Institute, 2004) noted:

> The percentage of time a paid staff coordinator devotes to volunteer management is positively related to the capacity of organizations to take on

additional volunteers. The best prepared and most effective volunteer programs are those with paid staff members who dedicate a substantial portion of their time to management of volunteers. This study demonstrated that, as staff time spent on volunteer management increased, adoption of volunteer management practices increased as well.

Another study of volunteers in Toronto (Toronto Community and Neighborhood Services, 2004) noted the consequence of not having a firm foundation:

> The agencies experiencing the greatest loss of volunteers were those with budget and program reductions. A quarter of these agencies had lost volunteers over the previous three years.

Their conclusion was simple and straightforward:

> It is neither realistic nor responsible to expect that once a volunteer is recruited they can work without ongoing support.

Organisations that involve volunteers can be paradoxical in their support for the concept of volunteering and their indifference towards its implementation. Hands for Nature (2002) examined volunteer management practices among community greening groups in Ontario and found that '90% of groups indicated that volunteers were either "extremely crucial" or "crucial" to the work they do. However, the majority of groups do not have a paid coordinator to support volunteers and 79% of groups do not train their staff to work with volunteers.'

The Points of Light Foundation (based in Washington DC, engaging and mobilising millions of volunteers) discovered a similar situation among national health agencies in 1996:

> Volunteer satisfaction with the agency was identified as the most important current issue for Voluntary Health Agencies (VHAs). All of the agencies reported that this issue was at least somewhat important, with over 90% indicating that this was a very or extremely important issue … when asked about the types of data collected by VHAs, only 31% reported that they collected data on volunteer satisfaction.

Brudney and Gazley (2002) found a similar incongruity among state coordinators of the USA Freedom Corps, who generally indicated that effective volunteer involvement would be essential to their programmatic success – meanwhile, 62% had not established any guidelines regarding volunteer management.

Perception versus reality

Fahey and Walker, in a study of volunteer ambulance officers in Tasmania (2001), note the differences that can occur between volunteers' perception of what good management support would be and the actual practices of the organisation:

Importance of management support and occurrence in last 12 months

	Important %	Has occurred %
• Management contact person being available and supportive	84	45
• Receiving training certificate	75	53
• Public relations work within area	70	31
• Social events organised by Volunteer Unit	68	37
• Receiving organisational information	67	28
• Opportunity to provide feedback to management	62	17
• Management staff visiting unit	61	38

The practices for increasing volunteer retention, which follow, are most likely to happen when they are the responsibility of a designated and empowered volunteer programme manager within the organisation.

Volunteers, like paid staff, are also sensitive to the overall operation of the organisation. As Clark (2003) commented, 'Sick organisations make people sick. A sick organization is one that feeds its volunteers and staff a steady diet of unexplained change, needless red tape, disorder, low or no recognition and little or no time for reflection.'

Do not waste the volunteer's time

Volunteering is a leisure activity, and leisure time is an increasingly rare and precious commodity. When volunteers offer their free time to help a charity, they are offering something of great value. If volunteers get the impression that their time is not valued by charity staff they will go and do something else. This is particularly likely to happen when volunteers feel their time is being wasted.

Volunteers may feel their time is being wasted for a variety of all-too-common reasons:

■ There is nothing for the volunteers to do when they arrive. Staff forget that they are coming or that there is no need for their service that day. In such cases, staff should either contact volunteers to tell them this before they travel to the workplace or prepare other, useful activities for them to work on for that day.

- The staff they were to meet are not prepared for them. When a volunteer is asked to be present at a certain time to work with staff on a given task, the staff should make sure they will indeed be ready to work on the task at that time.
- The resources or equipment that the volunteer needs are not available or do not work.
- The client the volunteer was to work with is not available and, although this was known in advance, the volunteer was not informed.
- Volunteers are given things to do that do not seem to be worthwhile or do not seem to be matched to their level of ability or interest.
- They spend a good portion of their time at the charity waiting for instructions or assignments.

A basic truism to remember is that no one volunteers simply to fill a hole in their day – people volunteer to do something *meaningful* during that empty time, something that makes a difference.

Let volunteers do work they want to do

Matching volunteers to appropriate assignments is a key to retention and motivation. People do not continue to volunteer for tasks that they neither enjoy nor are good at. Volunteers should only be asked to perform assignments in which they are interested and for which they are adequately prepared and supported.

Oddly enough, this obvious point is frequently overlooked by paid staff. A study of sports volunteering in Ontario (Ontario Ministry of Tourism and Recreation, 1990) reported that:

> Matching volunteers and tasks is an important motivational tool. It was not, however, identified by staff as a factor when motivation is low or as contributing to recruitment difficulties. This is an important concern as 'doing something I like' and 'feeling I accomplished something' are very important to 60% of volunteers.

People will volunteer for a short period to do practically anything, including work that does not suit them. They will not, however, generally continue this work any longer than they feel they have to, usually through a personal obligation to the person who asked them to volunteer. When that obligation is paid off, volunteers will cease volunteering unless what they are doing is motivating and rewarding.

Thank volunteers for their efforts

By far the most common management mistake is the failure to express appreciation to people for the work they do. This mistake is particularly critical when it comes to volunteers. If they sense that others do not appreciate their gift of time, they will take it elsewhere.

A simple 'thank you' (preferably with a smile) when volunteers leave can do wonders to keep them coming back. In addition, you might consider suggesting that all staff who work with volunteers keep these other easy methods of recognition in mind:

- Smile when you see them.
- Thank them for coming in.
- Write them a note.
- Tell them they've done a good job (but only if they have).
- Pass on any positive feedback about them from the people the charity serves.

Do not automatically assume that you have lost a volunteer

Some volunteers may simply become unconnected with an organisation. This is particularly easy to do when the volunteer commitment is one which comes and goes, without ongoing work or with periods in which the volunteer may not be in direct contact with the organisation. In such cases it is difficult to determine whether the volunteer has actively decided to leave the organisation or whether they are simply in a state of hiatus.

If the organisation does not reconnect volunteers – which can be easily done by contacting them and 're-inviting' them to participate – they will tend to drift away from the organisation and eventually cease to view themselves as volunteers. Many organisations make the mistake of assuming that volunteers who are not pushing forward to be involved do not want to be involved; they may simply be waiting to be asked. Ignoring these prospective 'lapsed' volunteers may be very common. Curtis (2000) noted about Australian Landcare volunteer efforts that 38% of groups in Corangamite and 42% of groups in Glenelg indicated that their group did not follow up with members when there was a pattern of absence from group activities, thus pre-emptively moving the member to the 'former volunteer' category without verifying that status with the volunteer.

McSweeney and Alexander (1996) noted:

> There may be times when a volunteer does not attend for a long period of time, perhaps due to illness, work or family pressures, or possibly

disillusionment with their role as a volunteer. Many volunteer managers feel uneasy making home visits, fearing that this may be seen as intrusive. Perhaps we could look at it from the volunteer's, or their family's, viewpoint. Your failure to make contact could well be interpreted as being uncaring or ungrateful for the services the member has given. Even in the most caring of organizations, it can be very difficult for an individual to gain the confidence to return after a lengthy break. Your contact could well prevent the loss of a valuable volunteer.

Osborne (2004) wrote about re-engaging volunteers who have separated from the organisation, in this case not from any decision of their own but because of being called up for military service, and noted that with this group:

> A returning service member should be allowed to feel needed but may not be ready for extensive volunteer duties. The normal and expected emotions will run the full spectrum of being on top of the world to carrying the full weight of the world. A slow and methodical re-engagement will provide a sense of being needed without over-commitment.

In most cases, reconnection is a distinct possibility for many 'lost' volunteers. How likely this reconnection may be is suggested by Fahey and Walker's (2001) finding that among volunteer ambulance officers in Tasmania who had resigned, 74% indicated that they would consider rejoining.

You might even take a very long view about re-inviting volunteers to participate. Some age groups – such as teens – may stop volunteering as they approach going to university. Many may even leave the community during that time, but return following graduation. Hosting an 'alumni reunion' party four years after they have departed gives them the opportunity to reconnect with the organisation; an opportunity they may not take on their own initiative.

Tillman (2002) wrote about the re-involvement of young volunteers in the Heritage Railways programme in the UK:

> Although many 16- to 18-year old volunteers drop out by their early twenties, they can make a positive contribution for 2 or 3 years. Moreover, some might become involved again in their 30s and later. For example, if 5 young people completed their work-experience activities each year, there would eventually be 150 'graduates' in their 30s–50s. If active encouragement resulted in 10% becoming involved again, there would be 15 experienced volunteers.

Dorsch et al (2002) summed up much of what we will discuss regarding the keys to volunteer retention. They noted that volunteers will generally exert more effort when they:

- like the social environment (psychological climate) where they volunteer
- want to achieve a desired outcome (volunteer motivation)
- feel that their volunteer role or link to the organisation is important (role identity and organisational identity)
- understand their role and accept its responsibilities (role clarity and role acceptance)
- feel sure they can carry out the role (role efficacy)
- feel good about volunteering (role satisfaction).

Alternatively, as Reilly (2004) put it:

> The more people have a positive experience as a volunteer, the more likely that they will continue to volunteer and the more likely that they will encourage people they know to become volunteers.

When volunteers fail to return

When volunteers end their service with an organisation, they will often say it is because their lives are very busy, that they have other commitments or that they just don't have the time. These excuses should be treated as such. They are commonly a substitute for the volunteer conveying more unpleasant facts – that the volunteer experience is unrewarding, that volunteering is too much of a hassle or that the volunteer does not trust the organisation. In fact, if the volunteer experience is sufficiently compelling, people will make the time to volunteer.

In the chapters that follow we will take a deeper look at the processes and management practices that can foster this retention.

WELCOMING VOLUNTEERS TO THE TEAM

In our book *Volunteer Management* (McCurley and Lynch, 1996) we referred to the research on self-esteem conducted by psychologists Harris Clemes and Reynold Bean. In their many books on this subject, these authors reported that people with high self-esteem are individuals who simultaneously satisfy a variety of motivational needs. One such need is a positive sense of connection with other people.

The importance of feeling connected

People who feel connected are those who experience a sense of belonging – a sense of being part of a relationship with others. In a highly mobile society, where friends and loved ones may live hundreds of miles away and the next door neighbour is sometimes a stranger, this need often goes unmet. People are left with feelings of isolation, dissatisfaction and loneliness. Psychologist William Glasser (1985) pointed out that the need for connection often exceeds even the need to survive, in that most people who try to commit suicide do so out of loneliness.

A sense of identification with a work group can meet this need and can result in healthier, happier individuals. Volunteers who feel a positive sense of connection with the staff and other volunteers of their agency will tend to feel good about the experience and will want to continue to volunteer.

Sadler and Marty (1998) noted of their study of volunteers in a US hospice programme:

> The use of the pronoun 'we' when referring to the hospice was common among all those interviewed ... Another common referent was to the climate of the training sessions, and how the staff treated training participants in a way that encouraged them to feel a 'part of the group'. In short, the hospice staff in this organization work hard to establish a common ground between the organization and the volunteers. This common ground is reflected in volunteers' pride of membership.

Based on a study of volunteers in AIDS organisations, Stewart and Weinstein (1997) found:

> Connection emerged as a major factor across the settings. At the social change setting, the connection was to the volunteers' gay male community, and/or a connection to 'the team', the work and project groups that characterized the setting. At the information/referral setting, there was also a connection to fellow volunteers, but respondents also spoke of a more abstract and impersonal connection to a social issue or to the diversity of the Bay Area. At the individual support setting the connection was without exception the one-on-one relationship with the client.

Unfortunately many non-profit and social service organisations inadvertently act in ways that dilute the connections that volunteers feel. Some of these actions are subtle; others are more blatant. All have the effect of making the volunteers feel separate from, and different to, paid staff. In such cases, the good feelings that volunteers might have about being an integral part of the agency are reduced, and the likelihood that they will elect to do something else with their leisure time increases.

Over the years we have collected a long list of such disconnecting factors. For simplicity, we have divided them into categories. These categories overlap with and support each other.

Things that disconnect volunteers

Susan Ellis, one of the publishing editors of *e-Volunteerism*, once said: 'Volunteer is a pay rate, not a job title.' One of the many implications of this insight is that volunteers should not be regarded as different from paid staff in any way except in their recompense and their hours. As is shown below, however, there are plenty of perceived differences that distinguish volunteers from paid staff, differences that make volunteers feel like outsiders rather than insiders and differences that work against a feeling of connection.

Differences in resources

In most charities volunteers do not have the use of dedicated workspace and equipment. They have nowhere to keep their work, to hang their coats or to place personal items which paid staff use to decorate their workplaces. In some charities they have no access to e-mail. Often, they are given nowhere to park their cars.

As a consequence, volunteers are made to feel that they are visitors to the agency rather than an integral part of the team. Of course, these 'perks' are expensive.

Allowing volunteers to have all of these things would not be cost-effective because most volunteers do not visit the agency on a daily basis. Not every volunteer can have their own office, computer or parking space. But many charities have found it possible to provide resources that volunteers can share, such as a desk, filing cabinets, a computer and their own e-mail accounts.

Volunteers who receive these resources feel much more valued and consequently more connected. Fahey and Walker (2001) reported on the consequences for volunteer ambulance officers (VAOs) in Tasmania of not having adequate resources, in this case in the form of uniforms suitable for female volunteers:

> The uniform design was a major issue for the female VAO. A one-piece coverall made toileting stops difficult, potentially embarrassing and cold (these stops are often at night in the bush). Most women identified that a two-piece uniform was necessary.

Phillips et al (2002), in a study of volunteers in Canada, reported that 17% of respondents surveyed noted 'lack of resources' as a way that organisations hindered their work as volunteers.

Differences in access to information

Another reason volunteers can feel detached is that they are not given the same information as paid staff. Management rarely shares information about problems or new directions with volunteers, rarely involves them in decision-making or invites them to staff meetings. Being excluded from the passing on of information makes volunteers feel separate and different from paid staff. When volunteers learn new things about the agency through the media or other secondary sources, they feel very left out.

Confidentiality is often the excuse made for keeping volunteers out of the information loop. One home for emotionally disturbed children, for example, kept the treatment goals of each child a secret from the volunteers because such information was supposed to be confidential. As a consequence, staff members were frequently upset when volunteers did things that worked against a treatment goal. This led to conflict between volunteers and paid staff because staff saw volunteers as 'screwing everything up'. When the agency allowed volunteers to be aware of the treatment goals for the children and to attend staff meetings where the children's progress was discussed, everything changed. As a result, volunteers could play an integral part in the progress of the child, conflicts between volunteer and paid staff diminished and, most importantly, the children's progress increased.

Volunteers should have equal access to the same information as is afforded paid staff. Paid staff members sometimes object to this, and argue that volunteers cannot be trusted with information. This argument appears to rely on the theory that there is something about being unpaid that makes a person inherently untrustworthy. There is no evidence to suggest that volunteers are any less trustworthy than other members of staff. If they are treated with trust, people, paid or unpaid, will react in a trustworthy fashion.

Differences in status

In many programmes paid staff members receive benefits and/or status-related distinctions that volunteers do not enjoy. In the extreme, there are 'staff only' signs prohibiting volunteers from entering certain areas or from doing certain things. In one animal shelter, for example, one staff member insisted 'Volunteers are not allowed to pet the puppies.' Distinctions also include not having a uniform or having a different uniform from that worn by paid staff. In some charities, paid staff wear name badges or business cards bearing their names, and volunteers either have none or have name badges or cards that simply say 'Volunteer'.

In some programmes staff members are given porcelain coffee cups while volunteers use styrofoam cups. Occasionally staff members receive discounts on items or events that volunteers do not. Another status-related difference is that volunteers sometimes receive a shorter and less complete induction and training than paid staff members. In one organisation with which we worked, volunteers were actually charged for training that employees received for free.

Tillman (2003) noted the following about the volunteers and staff of the National Aquarium in Baltimore:

> There is a meshing between the paid staff and unpaid staff, and sometimes it is hard to tell which is which. Even the uniforms of the paid and unpaid staff are the same. This familiarity certainly aids the retention of volunteers.

Status distinctions also result in the exclusion of volunteers from staff functions. These include both formal functions such as staff meetings and informal functions such as social gatherings. Volunteers who, for example, may not be invited to the staff Christmas party lose their sense of connection with the agency and with those employed by it. However, surprisingly, recognition events can contribute to a sense of being 'other'. Typically, there are no such similar events for paid staff. They are designated only for volunteers. Volunteers are frequently disappointed to find that staff members do not attend these volunteer recognition events.

Status distinctions extend even to the paid staff members who work with the volunteers. Frequently, the volunteer programme manager is one of the lowest status positions in the agency. When charities pay this person less than people in other management positions, equip them with hand-me-down computers and give them undesirable office space, they devalue the volunteer programme. Such actions communicate to everybody that volunteers are valued less highly than paid staff.

In their search for a sense of involvement, volunteers may seek out and bond with each other. This substitute for agency inclusion can cause more harm than benefit. The bonding between volunteers who feel like outsiders is often accompanied by a shared sense of injustice, a desire to band together to comfort each other in instances of unfair treatment. This creates an 'us versus them' mentality that is inherently divisive.

Status disparity is not an insurmountable problem and can be rectified through conscious acts of sensitivity to the feelings of all who work within an organisation. A simple example would apply to the recognition events referred to above. Instead of isolating volunteers for these events, charities could try having staff recognition events that honour both paid and unpaid staff. Such events would bear three advantages:

- Paid staff would receive formal recognition for their achievements (something that rarely happens anyway).
- Paid staff would attend the event.
- Volunteers would gain an enhanced sense of connection and equality.

Differences in authority

Volunteers are sometimes regarded as 'low down in the pecking order', and consequently are given little freedom to make decisions. This problem is often fed by a lack of direction. Volunteers who do not know what to do or how to do it lack the information and training needed to make the appropriate decisions about their work. When that happens, volunteers are in a very confused state. Consequently, they are perceived as individuals unable to make sensible decisions and are therefore never given the opportunity to do so.

This cycle results in inefficiency, frustration and wasted time and energy. At a hospital in southern California we talked to a group of teen volunteers who came to the hospital and spent most of their time sitting and waiting to be told what to do. To them, volunteering was an excruciatingly boring experience relieved only by the sense of resentment they felt at having their time treated as being of little value.

Where it does exists, this problem has its roots not only in the way volunteers are regarded, but also in the way volunteer positions are designed. Volunteers need to have their work defined with clear areas of responsibility and should be able to come to their assignments knowing what they are supposed to accomplish. With this knowledge, they can assess the situation and make a decision as to how to achieve their goals. Even the most inexperienced volunteers should not be deprived of the opportunity to contribute to the decision-making process. If they are inexperienced or unsure of the correct course of action, less seasoned volunteers can be encouraged to recommend a course of action to their supervisors.

Volunteer authority could also extend to the ability to make minor purchases for work items. This would communicate clearly to the volunteers that they are trusted and valued by the organisation. It would give the opposite message of being excluded from information. Rather than dividing, authority gives volunteers a sense of being part of the organisation.

In a study of volunteer firefighters, Thompson and Bono (1993) determined that 'over 90% of volunteer firefighters indicated that they were highly or moderately motivated by "being in control of what we do and how we do it" ... Only 4% indicated that control played no role in their motivation.'

Authority should extend beyond the boundaries of knowing what to do and how to do it. True authority vests in the recipient the ability to exercise creativity in pursuing desired goals. If volunteer positions are designed so that volunteers have clear goals to achieve, they can be encouraged to come up with new approaches to achieving them. If this idea makes staff nervous, this creative authority can extend simply to giving volunteers the ability to recommend new approaches. In this way, staff members can grant authority and encourage creativity without losing the confidence that volunteers' creative ideas will not create disaster.

Differences in rules

Formally or informally, volunteers often operate under different rules from those for paid staff. Leaving early, arriving late, taking personal telephone calls at work and such-like cause volunteers to distance themselves from paid staff.

The relaxed standards for attendance and conduct result in both benefit and detriment to those who take advantage of them. Clearly, these standards can be regarded as some of the advantages volunteers have over paid employees but, when volunteers live down to these lower standards, they diminish their own standing in the eyes of their paid counterparts. Paid staff members sometimes complain that volunteers are allowed to get away with things for which paid staff would be disciplined. The result is a cycle that leads to all kinds of disconnecting behaviours. Paid staff look down on those who do not appear to take their assignments seriously. Volunteers who get the impression that paid people have a low estimation of them feel alienated and consequently are not likely to stay around for very long.

Differences in expectation

A frequent mistake is not to demand much of volunteers in the erroneous belief that this will attract and retain volunteers in large numbers. However, if the volunteer position is one that anyone can do, and if the expectations are low, then volunteers will feel that neither they nor the group to which they are connected is very special.

Volunteers are often held to a lower standard than their paid colleagues. Sometimes, in fact, there is not much of a standard at all because volunteers often lack clearly defined job descriptions. This, coupled with the fact that they may receive less supervisory feedback than paid staff, means that volunteers feel that their work is valued less than that of others in the agency. When people realise others have low expectations of them, their self-esteem suffers.

Volunteers also feel low expectations on the all-too-common occasions when they arrive at the agency to discover there is nothing for them to do. Individuals who offer their precious time to an organisation automatically feel profoundly devalued when they are given nothing of value to do.

The expectations for volunteers as a group are just as crucial as those for each individual volunteer. People with a sense of involvement have a sense of 'we' as well as a sense of 'I'. The more special the 'we' is, the more special the individual feels as part of the group and the greater the self-esteem that is generated. High expectations for group performance translate to high group esteem and ultimately a positive sense of involvement for each individual member.

To foster self-esteem and a sense of involvement for their volunteers, some charities hold their volunteers to the same standards as those applied to paid staff. They clearly define the desired outcomes of the volunteers' positions and give them feedback as to how they are doing. By defining the position in terms of desirable outcomes, they enable volunteers to assign tasks to themselves. Again, the implications of Susan Ellis's dictum come into play: if paid staff treat volunteers as though they are a separate category, they will feel separate from the agency.

Differences in regard

Charities also sometimes give volunteers a sense of separation by regarding them as 'just volunteers'. This happens in many subtle ways, for example, paid staff may not know their names or remember the days when they are expected to work. Volunteers who perceive that the people with whom they work do not even care to know who they are will definitely not feel connected to the agency to which they have offered their time and energy.

Many of these differences come from the fact that volunteers do not come to work every day. In many programmes, in fact, volunteers work away from the office and are rarely seen. As a consequence, their paid colleagues do not get to know them. Some do not even learn their names or recognise their faces. When they meet, paid staff may fail to show basic friendliness such as smiling or engaging in conversation. In such circumstances volunteers are bound to feel invisible.

One idea to reduce this problem is to put pictures of all paid and unpaid staff on a notice board. Then if someone sees a volunteer and does not know who they are or what they do, they can go to the notice board and find out. This helps to connect people. It also gives everyone a strong sense that all who work there are equal (unless there is a separate section for volunteers).

Another difference in this regard stems from the time-honoured tradition of developing volunteer positions by asking staff for assignments they would like to see done by volunteers. In such circumstances staff will frequently identify things they personally do not like doing. A perfect example is the boring job of filing. Although filing is certainly a legitimate occupation for a volunteer, volunteers should not be confined to such tasks. If such a pattern should develop, paid staff will begin to assume that volunteers are people who are there to do the useful, ancillary services that no one else wants to do.

To counteract this scenario it is critical that volunteer programme managers make every effort to develop high value assignments for volunteers. Ask staff the question: 'What valuable thing could be done here that no one on the staff has the skills to do?' Answers to this question will lead to highly skilled positions for volunteers: assignments in fields such as graphic design, computer programming, public relations, strategic planning or accounting. When charities begin to involve volunteers in these fields, all volunteers are given more respect.

Individuals who are paid to provide highly professional services sometimes view volunteers as the people who do low-skilled work. Selig and Borton (1989) noted this effect among emergency medical services (EMS) volunteers in the US:

> Many EMS workers expressed concern about the working relationships they had with Emergency Department staff (nurses and doctors) as well as paramedics. One EMS volunteer said, 'It hurts when the ER [Emergency Room] staff throws away your run sheet.' Another volunteer said that often disparaging remarks are made by ER staff about field EMS providers. 'We never know how the patient was and what the diagnosis was ... we receive no feedback from the ER staff.'

Sometimes this misperception is attributable to nothing more than semantics. If we ask these people to 'volunteer', they may picture themselves doing menial or unskilled labour. They tend to react quite differently if they are asked to contribute their services on a '*pro bono* basis'. The term *pro bono* (for the public good) is one that has a positive connotation in the minds of professionals. If paid staff are encouraged to consider volunteers as the agency's '*pro bono* workers' they may ultimately treat the volunteers with a higher level of regard. We have often thought that volunteer programmes would receive more respect if the manager's title were 'Director of *Pro Bono* Resources'.

Creating a positive sense of connection

A positive feeling of connection can be enhanced in volunteer programmes by many leadership actions, some of which have been referred to earlier in this chapter.

What follows are some of the most powerful ways to establish a feeling of belonging.

Creating a welcoming atmosphere for new volunteers

A sense of connection and bonding is easily established or diminished by first experiences in a new setting. One way to enhance an immediate sense of connection is to have a welcoming ceremony for new volunteers. This can be done during an induction, when volunteers are officially greeted and informed about the organisation in an official way. It can also be done through an informal ceremony on the volunteer's first day of work, either through a personal greeting, or a phone call if they are not in an office setting.

As simple as this seems, such a welcome provides the official imprint of acceptance by the charity and establishes in the mind of the volunteer that they have truly become a part of the organisational team. If volunteers work in departments outside the direct control of the volunteer programme manager, then walking them down to the appropriate department on their first working day and introducing them to those with whom they will be working can also create this sense of welcome.

This welcome can be enhanced through the granting of organisational symbols – a business card, T-shirt with corporate logo, designated workspace, e-mail address and so on – anything which physically communicates the notion that the volunteer has become a part of the team.

As the Federal Emergency Management Association (FEMA) (1995) noted:

> Symbols of belonging to a group or organization are important reinforcers of allegiance and membership. Uniforms, caps, insignias, or logos on equipment and clothing promote loyalty and a sense of belonging to the group.

The importance of food must not be overlooked, as noted by Reilly (2004):

> Volunteer experiences could be improved generally, with the provision of basic services such as tea- and coffee-making facilities for the volunteers.

Seeking volunteer input and participation

Ask volunteers for their ideas about how the agency might improve. Volunteers often see many opportunities to enhance the services or the internal systems of an agency. In fact, because they are often new to the agency, they are uniquely suited to recognising such opportunities. Their views are less constrained than those of paid staff, who tend to take the systems for granted and accept them as given. Volunteers, coming in from the outside, sometimes look at the way an organisation does things and think 'That's silly. I wonder why they do it that way.' Lee and Catagnus (1999) noted that '... often volunteers see things that paid staff don't see simply because paid staff are so used to the way things are.'

Often, however, volunteers do not air their opinions because they fear that their insights are based on ignorance of facts which they do not yet appreciate. Counteract this reticence by asking them for their input. If you can then help them to be champions of their good ideas and get the suggestions put into practice, volunteers will inevitably develop a profound sense of identification with the agency. After all, it is 'their agency' if some of the agency practices come directly from them. The Canadian Museums Association (2001) commented:

> There is a general view by volunteers that they must and should have a meaningful say in the development and direction of policies and programs that affect their responsibilities. This is more than a matter of mere form. It is recognition of the volunteer's value to the organization. As well, it opens the door to valuable ideas and insights from the front line of community contact, thereby helping to ensure a relevant public message.

Another fundamental means of creating a feeling of connectedness is to invite volunteers to attend and participate in work-related and social functions. Any kind of social or work-related invitation will have this effect. Invite volunteers to parties, meetings and training sessions but do not stop with attendance. Invite volunteers to participate in these functions and to share their ideas. Invitations are a great connector. They communicate esteem and respect. They also reinforce the importance of the volunteer's role in the agency.

Cravens (2003) listed a variety of ways to obtain quick input from volunteers on their experience and on organisational practices, including:

- On-the-spot surveys following meetings, training sessions and events.
- Stamped postcard surveys.
- Walking-around informal surveys.
- Once-a-year e-mail survey.
- Feedback system on web page.
- Exit interviews of departing volunteers.

Communicating volunteer contributions

When work is done well, leaders should do more than privately compliment the volunteer(s) who accomplished it. Leaders at all levels in the agency should spread the word about positive volunteer achievements. They should talk about the values and standards of the organisation and what it means to be part of the group. When a volunteer makes a good decision (assuming things are set up to allow volunteers to make decisions at all) the volunteer programme manager can say something like 'That was the right thing to do.' They can then tell other volunteers about this, saying something like 'That's the kind of thing we do in this agency.' Such a statement makes everyone feel worthwhile and proud to be part of the organisation.

We can also help volunteers to identify with the agency by making sure they know the mission of the organisation and, above all, how their work relates to achieving that mission. Nothing is as fundamental to a team's effectiveness as a common sense of what the team is collectively trying to achieve. Staff and volunteers should see themselves as equal partners in pursuing this goal. At one hospital, for example, volunteers are told that the mission of the hospital is to reduce the suffering of patients. These volunteers are also told how their work applies to that mission – so the hospitality cart volunteers know they help to cheer people up and reduce their anxiety; those who transport specimens know they are helping to find out what is wrong with the patient so that their suffering can be treated; and those who give information to visitors know they are helping to cheer up the patient by directing their visitors to them. When people see their work as directly relating to the mission, it gives them a sense of purpose and a sense of identification with the work of the whole organisation.

Identifying volunteers by name, title and dress

One of the fundamental ways of producing a feeling of connectedness is as simple as calling volunteers by name. This cannot be accomplished unless staff members understand the importance of learning the names of their volunteers. In situations involving large numbers of volunteers, recognition can be aided with mnemonic devices such as nametags or a notice board showing the names and pictures of all paid and volunteer personnel.

Titles are also a way to give a volunteer a sense of status and place. Consider the implications of simply introducing someone at a meeting as a 'volunteer'. What does this say about their role, contribution or place in the organisation? Titles for volunteers, like titles for paid staff, should give some indication of the titleholder's area of work and responsibility. This title helps communicate their role in, and contribution to, the organisation and its work.

Dress codes are also important in establishing a sense of shared identity. When volunteers and paid staff have similar dress codes it tends to strengthen a sense of equality. And it can be fun, as illustrated at the Burning Man event (an annual eight-day arts festival in the Nevada desert):

> While most departments do not ask their volunteers to wear uniforms, there are a few exceptions. The Black Rock Rangers wear khaki, DPW (Department of Public Works) wears T-shirts, Media Mecca volunteers don silver cowboy hats when on duty, the Lamplighters wear robes during the nightly Lighting Ceremony, and the people who volunteer at the gate wear T-shirts.

Uniforms can be a significant way to make volunteers feel as if they belong, especially if the uniforms themselves have a sense of significance to the volunteer. Aldridge (2003) commented on the impact of uniforms among fire brigade volunteers in Australia:

> In my experience when a volunteer joins a brigade the sooner they get a uniform, the higher the chances are of retaining their services. Quickly providing a new volunteer with a uniform not only is a sign of acceptance but makes the volunteer feel welcome and a part of the team, thus increasing motivation and enthusiasm ... It's surprising how a $30 brigade T-shirt can impact upon the motivation of a new member.

This effect can be so powerful that changes in the uniform can have an impact on volunteer participation. Cheng (1998) reported on the effects on retention by the Civil Air Patrol (CAP) of changing the uniforms of its volunteer members away from uniforms that strongly resembled those worn by the US Air Force:

> While the CAP does not perform exit interviews of quitters or empirically study its turnover problem (to do so would be too threatening to 'career advancement'), I asked ten unit commanders to compare how much turnover they had one year prior to and one year after the uniform change. The period of a membership is one year. They said they had lost from 10–20

percent of their membership within one year of the uniform change. They also estimated that another 10–20 percent became inactive.

Encouraging volunteer creativity

As noted above, volunteers should have the same opportunity for input as paid staff. It is not enough, however, to listen to the input without using it. Adopting this input may require abandoning established, comfortable methods for untested waters. Organisations that are willing to take the chance and learn from their volunteers unleash a tremendous amount of innovation and service improvement. The testing and experimentation that result from this innovation are of themselves a potential bonding tool. People who engage in new experiences together experience a sense of connectedness. By insisting passionately on constant innovation and improvement, leaders encourage people to try out new ways of doing things. When the new techniques and methods are experienced by teams the sense of connectedness is enhanced even more.

Volunteers who feel they have a role in the decision-making process develop an enhanced sense of connection with the group. To encourage and foster volunteer input, leaders must take great care to hide their biases and opinions. Group members who know what the person in authority wants may tend to support that position and will not, therefore, truly participate in the process. Without true participation, there cannot be a genuine sense of connection. Leaders who, for whatever reason, cannot accept volunteer input should be honest with their personnel instead of soliciting input they have no intention of using.

Setting high standards

In developing positions for volunteers (other than for one-time volunteers whom you do not expect to retain), avoid setting performance standards that are too low. If the expectations are too easy to meet, people will not feel special about their participation. Volunteers should not have lower standards than those of paid staff.

Clark and Shimoni (2002a) noted:

> Agencies sometimes hesitate to demand accountability from busy professionals who are volunteering their time. However, participants in our study felt that accountability was crucial and that accountability mechanisms should be built into the terms of reference for volunteer positions. In the long run, it was felt that everyone's time would be more effectively used if expectations were clearer.

Monitoring volunteer regard

One of the volunteer programme manager's assigned responsibilities should involve monitoring behaviour that inadvertently excludes volunteers. The manager should, for example, take note of meetings to which volunteers are not invited, especially if such exclusions result not from deliberate action but because no one thought to offer volunteers the opportunity to attend. With such monitoring, managers can take the necessary action to prevent volunteers from feeling like second-class citizens.

Not only should the leaders of volunteer programmes scrutinise the views of paid staff members, they should also monitor the volunteers' views of themselves. Managers should listen for comments volunteers make about the expectations they have of themselves and their co-workers. If people say things like 'I'm just a volunteer', or 'What do they expect for free?' it should cause alarm bells to ring. People's self-esteem falls when they regard themselves as part of a below-average group. This negative sense of connectedness leads to a high turnover of staff and volunteers. Upon hearing negative statements such as this, leaders should try to generate positive ideas for improving the situation. They might ask: 'What makes you say that? What can you do to improve this situation? What sort of place would you want to work in? What can you do to make this organisation more like the kind of place you want it to be?'

Giving volunteers ownership in the mission

When working with staff to develop positions for volunteers, the volunteer programme manager should make sure that volunteers (or teams of volunteers) have a sense of ownership of a client or project. Volunteers should be able to point to something and say: 'This is mine.' This possessive relationship could extend to a client or to a programme, such as Big Brothers Big Sisters (the international volunteer agency that mentors children), or a tutoring programme. Alternatively, volunteers could claim ownership of a particular product or geographic service area. Only when there is ownership can people be proud of their work. Fragmentation of ownership also generates blame and criticism, and criticism is the prime enemy of any feelings of belonging.

Gooch (2003), in a study of ecological volunteers in Australia, noted the significance of geographic ownership for retention:

> Many of the participants in this study derive their identity from their ecological surroundings, and this is further strengthened by their voluntary activities. This study revealed that having an ecological identity can be a strong motivator for further volunteering. Creating a 'sense of place' and fostering ecological identity can be one way of building on the existing

positive impacts of catchment care groups, and encouraging long-term volunteering in local areas.

Offering sincere and consistent recognition

The volunteer programme manager should encourage paid staff to celebrate the accomplishments of volunteers in the context of their contribution to the goals of the group. Recognition must be consistent so that people do not suspect favouritism. Team accomplishments can also be celebrated, giving equal credit to all team members. When recognition is given to a team consisting of both paid staff and volunteers, the sense of connection is very powerful. The next chapter deals with this in detail.

Promoting interaction

Because it is impossible for people to feel connected without interaction, volunteer programme managers should look for opportunities to promote interaction among group members. This is particularly important where there are few 'natural' opportunities for people to share their common experiences, for example, in friendly visitor and literacy programmes, volunteers work with clients on independent timetables. Volunteers work with little daily supervision and rarely appear in the office.

Effective volunteer supervisors, knowing that 'it's lonely out there', take pains to bring their people together for training, potluck suppers and other events where they can share their 'war stories'. Such events are also opportunities for the staff to share relevant information with the volunteers. All these techniques enable volunteers to enhance their sense of involvement.

Tillman (2003) noted the importance of promoting social interaction in a discussion of the volunteer programme of the National Aquarium in Baltimore, considered one of the best volunteer programmes in the US:

> The groups of shifts of people who work together are cohesive. Members of each shift celebrate birthdays and provide support for each other in times of ill health or even death. The Volunteer Lounge has a coffee table that's laden with baked goods and other treats that people often bring in to share. We even have our own cookbook – a compilation of favorite recipes. Volunteers are encouraged to know each other as people, not just as work colleagues.

Creating this sense of intimacy and connection can be more difficult as an organisation becomes larger. Field and Johnson (1993) noted the changes that volunteers perceived in LOROS (the Leicestershire and Rutland Organisation for the Relief of Suffering), a hospice programme in the UK, as the charity became larger and more successful:

> LOROS has grown from a small, tightly focused organisation, dependent on a relatively small group of committed volunteers, to a much larger, busier, more diverse and geographically dispersed organisation, dependent upon a large pool of volunteers. These changes in the organisation had affected the way in which some volunteers experienced their work, and although they were supportive of the expansion of the organisation their sense of intimacy and belonging had lessened.

Sport England (2003), in a study of volunteers in sports, found an interesting aspect of the difficulty of linking some types of volunteer positions into the general social network:

> Another worry here is that players are showing less and less respect for officials and the enjoyment is going out of refereeing, umpiring and judging. One hockey club commented 'umpiring is a very unloved position and over the last three years it has got a lot worse ... umpires don't get the camaraderie, no one talks to them afterwards.'

Listening and learning

Finally, people feel a stronger sense of belonging when others listen to them. Be sincere in trying to understand volunteers' points of view. Get to know as much about them as time allows. People feel more connected to a programme where they believe that people are interested in what they have to say.

Many of the elements above relate to the issue of communication between the volunteer and the organisation. This communication is not always perceived as effective. Phillips et al (2002) noted in a study of Canadian volunteers:

> When we compare the type of support volunteers say they are provided with to what they say it would take to retain them as volunteers, it appears that the main shortcoming is ineffective communication. While 48% of volunteers in this study said that communication and responsiveness are vital to retaining volunteers, only 12% noted that such support was forthcoming from their organizations.

The National Mentoring Center (Public/Private Ventures, 2001) recommended the following pattern of communication with volunteer mentors:

1   Contact the mentor within the first two weeks of the match. Use this contact to make sure the pair is meeting, to find out what activities they have done together, and to assess how the mentor feels about the match thus far.

2   During the next few months, continue to check in with the mentor every two weeks. These ongoing contacts will help ensure that the mentor and youth meet regularly, and they are important for uncovering any start-up problems that require programme staff's immediate assistance. (Many school-based mentoring programmes keep track of how frequently each pair is meeting by having a logbook at the school where mentors sign in. However, it is still essential to have regular instances of telephone or face-to-face contact to discuss the match.)

3   For at least a year, continue to check in monthly with the mentor. The check-in discussions during this period can be more focused on monitoring the quality of the match relationship, assessing whether it is making progress toward its goals, learning whether the mentor or youth is losing interest in the match, and helping to address problems that may be arising between the pair. Your programme should also make sure that mentors know how to contact staff, whenever necessary, for advice and support.

The above listing is designed to show the variety of ways in which volunteers can be made to feel welcome, equal and involved. The goal is to reach a point such as that described in the Impact Study of Volunteers at the 2002 Commonwealth Games in the United Kingdom (International Centre for Research and Consultancy for the Tourism and Hospitality Industries, 2003):

> At the beginning of the Games, many volunteers found they were concerned about what was being expected of them. This was dispelled for most as the Games progressed. The overwhelming feeling was one of comradeship, teamwork and embarking on a special experience with like-minded people.

The relationship between work and a sense of belonging

While much of fostering feelings of belonging deals with personal relationships, it is also important to note that volunteers must be connected to the organisation through their work. Designing an effective role for volunteers is discussed in somewhat greater detail in Chapter 5. However, work is also important in fostering a sense of involvement for volunteers, sometimes in a way that is obvious, yet easily overlooked. The work that volunteers contribute is their way of establishing a connection to the organisation. To feel that this has been done, and that they have made a difference, volunteers must have enough 'work' to do in order to feel they have made a difference. The implication of this simple point is that asking a volunteer to do too little can tend to result in the loss of a sense of involvement and cause retention problems just as much as asking a volunteer to do too much can cause burnout. Hanawi (1990) commented:

> There is a minimal level of activity which is necessary for volunteers to feel connected to an organization; there are individual variations in this critical level but certainly when a person's involvement falls below one or two hours a month, or when there is no continuity in the level of contact, volunteers will drift away.

Volunteers who are not engaged in assignments on a regular basis should have other means of interaction with the organisation. These could include receiving newsletters, participating in listserv discussions (e-mail exchange) or training sessions with other volunteers and receiving periodic telephone contact from the volunteer manager.

Building a network of connections

The suggestions above are designed to show ways to build connections between the volunteer and the organisation. Since this is necessarily a set of connections among human beings, it might be useful to conclude this chapter by briefly discussing to whom these connections should be made.

There are four options:

- clients with whom the volunteers interact
- staff with whom the volunteers work
- other volunteers
- the volunteer programme manager.

Connections should be established with each of these groups.

Clients serve as a reminder to volunteers of the work they are doing and the need for that work. Feedback from clients about the work done by the volunteer is one of the most powerful forms of volunteer recognition – a direct expression of thanks from the person being helped. Especially in programmes where volunteers work directly with clients, reminding clients simply to thank volunteers can have a powerful effect.

Staff are co-workers with the volunteers and fellow members of the team of service providers. The respect of co-workers has long been recognised as a significant factor in building organisational commitment.

Other **volunteers** represent the connection to peers; a relationship with others of similar interest and dedication. Many organisations create intentional networks of volunteers through either 'buddy' systems or 'discussion teams', which are mechanisms that allow volunteers to share their experiences with other volunteers and to meet friends.

Ogilvie (2004) noted the use of this system among homeless shelter programmes in New York City:

> In all of the shelters, the other common way to begin training a new volunteer is to partner them with a veteran volunteer. This partnership will last for at least a few months, and after that the not-so-new volunteers learn the subtleties of the job, and they begin to be socialized into the shelter.

Fraser and Gottlieb (2001) commented on these feelings of connection in a study of volunteers in long-term care organisations in Ontario, Canada:

> Among the sources of satisfaction and personal reward associated with volunteering, the majority spoke first and foremost about the relationships they had formed with clients, staff, and other volunteers. Day program volunteers in particular talked about the sense of connection and belonging they gained from their association with a particular program and setting, whereas those providing friendly visiting and escorted transportation underscored the self-satisfaction they gained from rendering services that they felt were essential for the very survival of their clients. One volunteer took great pride in the fact that certain clients specifically requested her as their volunteer driver, while another stated that she always felt welcomed as though she were an old friend when she entered her agency.

One excellent method of connecting volunteers to other volunteers is through formally creating mentoring relationships between new and more experienced volunteers. This has been done successfully in the Master Gardener Volunteer Programme with positive results on volunteer retention. Rogers (1997) commented on the success of a programme in Oregon that matched mentors with newcomer volunteers – the mentors phoned to welcome new volunteers to the programme, reminded them of forthcoming training events and spent time with them during the first training class. The mentors also worked beside the newcomers during their first workdays. The results have been impressive:

> Retention of new members has been much higher since the mentor program was introduced. Before the program was introduced in 1993 approximately 50% of the new volunteers completed the class and their voluntary service commitment. Since 1993, 38 of 51 or 75% of volunteers have completed their

commitments and many have gone well beyond the minimum commitment of time.

Phillips and Bradshaw (1999) reported on the success of a similar effort in Florida:

> Drop-out rates for the three annual Master Gardener basic training programs prior to the Mentor program were 26%, 17% and 27% for the years 1995, 1996 and 1997, respectively. While the 1998 class in Pinellas County was one-third smaller than the previous years, the trainee drop-out rate for the basic training program was 2%.

Fryar (2004) commented on the advantages of forming social clubs among volunteers:

> Volunteer social clubs can:
> - provide a great opportunity for volunteers to share their workplace and experiences with families and friends (which may in turn lead some of these individuals to become volunteers with your agency)
> - offer the chance for volunteers to get to know one another outside of their regular volunteer routine
> - allow a medium for volunteers from different areas to meet one another
> - enable volunteers to meet new people and experience new things.

Finally, the volunteer programme manager is a connection point for volunteers, especially when he or she is the paid staff member who has the most contact with volunteers on a daily basis. Many managers refer to a portion of their job commonly know as 'mothering', taking the time to relate to volunteers who need a personal connection with the organisation. This is a time-consuming but invaluable use of a programme manager's time.

In general, effort should be made to foster connections with all of the above groups. The most common mistake is only to create a connection between the volunteer programme manager and the volunteer. The error of this approach is revealed if the volunteer programme manager leaves or retires from that position. The longer they have been involved, the more revered they were and the more volunteers who were primarily 'bonded' with them, the more likely it is that volunteers will also choose to depart when the volunteer programme manager leaves. Many new volunteer programme managers have experienced this 'volunteer flight' without realising that it was nothing to do with them – they were simply the victims of an over-concentration of bonding in one individual and a subsequent shattering of the bonds to the organisation upon that person's departure.

Some bonding connections may need to be discouraged in the case of some types of volunteer positions. Nelson et al (2004b) reported on the need among long-term volunteer ombudsmen to control some relationships that might be formed by the volunteers:

> Opportunities for friendship, personal development, and support are also important, but these needs must be assessed and fostered within the context of the program's advocacy mission. For instance, managers should structure affiliation opportunities that reinforce desirable role behavior (partisan advocacy) – by providing social opportunities, policies and training that encourage bonding among and between ombudsmen and residents. Conversely, they should discourage friendships between volunteers and facility staff. Such relationships may sensitize volunteers to facility values, thus undermining their resident-centered role.

Farmer and Fedor (2001) affirmed the above comments on establishing networking bonds and suggested one further possibility when they noted:

> ... we found some support for the idea that social interaction among volunteers would have salutary effects on voluntary contributions. This implies the importance of not letting volunteers become isolated by building a social web that encourages volunteers to stay engaged. According to these data, voluntary organizations could better capitalize on recruiting volunteers who work at the same for-pay organizations as a recruiting strategy to increase social contact and cohesion.

The impact of building connective bonds and friendship cannot be overstated. A study by AARP (American Association of Retired Persons) in 2004 found that 63% of volunteers reported 'develop new friendships' as a motivation for volunteering and 53% listed 'fun/socialising.' Ilsley (1990) noted that in the case of long-term volunteers, the friendships they develop have become the primary reason for many to continue volunteering.

In the long run, the connections that volunteers form with others in the organisation will be one of the strongest ways of bonding the volunteer to the organisation – creating a network that both creates and sustains the relationship over time.

chapter 4

MAKING VOLUNTEERS FEEL SPECIAL

In addition to feeling connected to the charity and the people who work there, volunteers' self-esteem is underpinned by a feeling that they have a unique combination of characteristics – abilities, personality traits, eccentricities, beliefs, quirks and style – that make them uniquely who they are. One of the reasons people do not often feel high self-esteem is that there is a conflict between the need for connection and the need for uniqueness.

Sometimes this conflict occurs because a charity needs people to conform to a certain standard of behaviour. When that happens, volunteers will have to choose between conforming for the sake of being accepted (and hence feeling connected) and being true to themselves. A volunteer, for example, might feel that if they express their true feelings in a group discussion, the group will regard them as a maverick or an odd person. The desire to be connected is thus in conflict with the need to express their individuality.

Given the choice between feeling connected or unique, people tend to compromise. To take a minor example, if the charity has a dress code which conflicts with the volunteer's sense of style, the volunteer may compromise by conforming to the code some of the time or only partially. When people compromise in this way, they do not feel fully connected or unique.

Some methods to enhance a volunteer's sense of being unique follow, together with some methods to help them overcome the conflict with the need for the feeling of belonging.

Providing validations to volunteers

One method to enhance volunteers' sense of uniqueness is to praise them for their personality traits. These validations tend to make a volunteer feel good. And the sense of feeling appreciated that is fostered also makes them feel connected.

A validation is a statement that praises a person's positive characteristics. Examples of validations include:

- I admire your work ethic.
- I'm impressed at how pleasant you are after a hard day.
- You are certainly quick.
- I love your sense of humour.
- You are so good at solving problems.
- I like the way you stay calm in the face of conflict.
- You are such a caring person.

Such statements can be made at any time, without the volunteer having done anything in particular. They are recognition not for the work they do but for the kind of people they are.

Validations are very powerful statements. People are not used to hearing such comments. Some of us have been trained not to make such statements to another person. Oddly, people who feel totally uncomfortable saying something like 'You always come up with good ideas' have no difficulty saying 'You are a brainless idiot.' As a consequence, keep in mind that a little of this goes a long way and that it is easy to overdo it.

In their simplest form, validations begin with phrases such as:

- You are ...
- You always ...

Such statements would be followed by a positive personality trait. For example:

- You are certainly quick.
- You always come up with good ideas.
- You are the hardest worker I've ever seen.

The technical term for this approach in psychology is altercasting; attributing a positive characteristic to someone as a way of motivating them actually to exhibit the characteristic.

Validations are even more connecting if they begin with the word 'I'. For example:

- I admire ...
- I'm impressed by ...
- I like ...
- I value ...
- I treasure ...

Again these phrases are followed by a mention of the trait being praised:

- I admire how pleasant you are at the end of a stressful day.
- I'm impressed by your ability to stick to a task.
- I like the way you keep an even temper.
- I value your keen insight.
- I treasure your cheerfulness.

Because it is likely your volunteers will not have heard many validations in their lives, you should be careful not to overdo it. But once people get used to hearing these kinds of statements from you, they might become comfortable about validating each other. A mutually validating environment is one in which people feel connected and unique at the same time.

One charity executive helped this process to get started by handing all of her people a list of the names of all the group members. Next to each name, she asked them to write a positive quality they perceived in that person. She then compiled the results, giving each person a list of all the positive qualities the others had identified in them. Morale instantly improved and people became more accepting of each other as members. By knowing that the rest of the group valued their personal qualities, people were able to feel both connected and unique.

Matching volunteers to assignments

Another way to enhance volunteers' sense of uniqueness is to put them in a position where their strengths can shine. Volunteers who are quite personable, for example, might be put in a position in which they interact with the public rather than working on computers (unless, of course, they would much rather work with computers – the volunteer's wishes should be the primary concern).

Many organisations take a casual attitude towards assessing the work interests of volunteers, assuming that they will be willing to help in whatever positions they are most needed, and then suffer accordingly as disinterested volunteers begin not to show up for work. This effect may be exacerbated during volunteer interviewing because many volunteers unfamiliar with the type of work done by the organisation may simply express an interest in 'helping', since that is their primary reason for offering to volunteer.

The situation may be additionally complicated because volunteers will react not only to the type of work they are doing but also to the person for whom they are doing it. This is especially true when volunteers are in positions where they are assisting a particular client over a period – in this situation the client and their relationship with the volunteer become an important part of the work situation. Fraser and Gottlieb (2001) noted the potential implications of this for matching volunteers to positions, based on a study of a group of friendship volunteers assigned to work with senior citizens in long-term care situations:

> Volunteers who are seeking to form a personal relationship with clients will be disappointed if they find themselves assigned to a client who is cognitively impaired, disoriented, or otherwise incapable of achieving rapport. For

example, the staff of the K-W Friendship Group for Seniors has recognized that the clients can be so disabled and elderly that the volunteers cannot form personal relationships with them. Hence, if they wish to prevent the volunteer from leaving the organization, they must conduct a careful assessment of what the volunteer is seeking, what the volunteer can offer, and what the client needs and can offer to the volunteer. Given the increasing complexity of the matchmaking process, it becomes even more important for agency staff to conduct an assessment at the client's home, and to accompany the volunteer to the initial home visit to ensure that the match is suitable. When it comes to matching needy volunteers to needy clients, no longer does 'one size fit all' or even most.

Tschirhart et al (2001) noted that determining the motivational goal of a volunteer is not only important as an indicator of what type of work a volunteer would enjoy but also influences how a volunteer will go about doing that type of work:

Goals guide behavior. Identifying a potential volunteer's goals can help in predicting the types of activities he or she will emphasize while performing a service role. For example, a volunteer with a strong social goal is likely to spend more time and effort making friends than a volunteer whose social goal is weaker.

Fischer and Shaffer (1993) noted another important point that should be kept in mind. Referring to a study of women who volunteer for the League of Women Voters that indicated a major reason given for continuing volunteering was 'finding the work interesting', they commented:

What is notable is that the appeal of interesting work was much more likely to be given as a reason for staying active than for joining the organization.

Volunteers are not likely to continue volunteering for positions where they do not enjoy the type of work or do not feel qualified to perform the work. This discomfort will tend to increase the longer the volunteer is in the unsatisfying position and the volunteer is likely to alleviate the difficulty by departing.

Paying careful attention to the needs and interests of volunteers during the initial volunteer interview is the key to successful placement, since it allows for the customisation of volunteer positions to the individual interests and character of each volunteer.

Gidron (1984) noted:

Organizationally, this individualisation of tasks requires a careful placement of the volunteer in the job, based on the special needs and talents of the volunteer. This, in turn, suggests that the volunteer coordinator possesses thorough and accurate personal information on volunteers. It also suggests a periodic review of the volunteer's attitudes to his/her work, and if need be, enriching it or changing it.

By placing volunteers in work where they can take advantage of their strengths, we provide others with natural opportunities to appreciate the volunteer's uniqueness. Validations are more likely to happen in such circumstances.

Recognising volunteers' accomplishments

Another way to enhance volunteers' sense of being special is to express appreciation for their unique contributions to the charity. By letting people know we appreciate their voluntary efforts on our behalf, we help them keep a sense that it is worth it to come back.

Reward systems help in a variety of ways:

- They establish a cultural norm that fosters accomplishment and achievement.
- They clarify expectations among new volunteers as to what might be expected of them.
- They honour those who contribute to and help accomplish the mission of the organisation.

Many charities have formal programmes of recognition. These sometimes have the drawback, however, of giving everyone the same token of appreciation. To make recognition really meaningful to our volunteers, we have to get to know them as individuals and express our appreciation for their efforts in a way they find satisfying. To take a minor example, if you know someone loves coffee, giving them a gift certificate to Starbucks may be an appropriate way to express your appreciation. This may not satisfy another volunteer, however, who thinks that Starbucks is a greedy corporation oppressing the world's poor.

Matching recognition to types of volunteers

Getting to know each volunteer can be difficult in large charities where no single member of staff can personally know all the volunteers. In such circumstances, you might have some knowledge about individuals but not enough to gauge their individual tastes and preferences. Fortunately, it is also possible to think about systems of volunteer recognition that are appropriate to particular types of volunteers, thus allowing a programme to make educated guesses about recognition items that would be appropriate and welcomed by entire categories of volunteers.

We will consider three different ways of thinking about providing recognition items to volunteers:

■ By varying levels of intensity – daily, intermediate and major
■ By motivational orientation of the volunteer – achievement, affiliation or power
■ By style of volunteering – short-term or long-term.

Levels of intensity

Here we match the effort we put in to recognising the volunteer with the level of accomplishment that we are praising them for. Someone who shows up to do the work and who completes it routinely, for example, might receive verbal praise such as 'Thanks for coming in today.' If a volunteer brings in a million pounds to your cash-starved charity, on the other hand, they should be praised in a more labour-intensive way, such as arranging a meal in their honour. What follows are some examples of different levels of recognition activity.

Daily means of providing recognition

■ Saying 'Thank you'
■ Telling volunteers they have done a good job
■ Suggesting volunteers join you for coffee
■ Asking for their opinions
■ Greeting volunteers when they arrive in the morning
■ Showing interest in their personal interests
■ Smiling when you see them
■ Building them up to your boss (in their presence)
■ Jotting small thank-you notes to them
■ Having a refreshment with volunteers after work
■ Saying something positive about a volunteer's personal qualities
■ Telling volunteers what has happened at the organisation since their last visit

Intermediate means of providing recognition

■ Taking volunteers to lunch
■ Providing food at volunteer meetings
■ Letting volunteers put their names on the products they produce
■ Writing them a letter of commendation (with copies for the human resources file and other appropriate people)
■ Putting volunteers on important task forces or committees

- Giving the volunteers' best parking space to the 'volunteer of the month'
- Putting up graphic displays showing progress towards targets
- Mentioning major contributors by name in your status reports to upper management
- Inviting volunteers to present their results to more senior members of staff
- Giving volunteers permission to go to a seminar, convention or professional meeting, if possible at the organisation's expense
- Writing articles about their performance for newsletters or newspapers
- Having volunteers present a training session to co-workers
- Decorating volunteers' work areas on their birthday
- Asking your boss to write volunteers a letter of thanks
- Celebrating the major accomplishments of a volunteer
- Letting volunteers represent you at important meetings
- Putting their picture on the notice board with news of their accomplishments
- Cutting out articles and cartoons volunteers might be interested in
- Organising informal chats with organisation leadership

Major means of providing recognition

- Making special caps, shirts, belt buckles or lapel badges honouring the group
- Encouraging volunteers to write an article about some accomplishment at work
- Giving a plaque, certificate, or trophy for being best team or crew, most improved results and so on
- Offering tuition assistance to volunteers
- Buying volunteers good equipment
- Having a volunteer's picture in the paper for outstanding accomplishment
- Giving volunteers additional responsibilities and new titles
- Renting newspaper space to thank volunteers
- Putting up a banner celebrating a major accomplishment
- Honouring a volunteer for years of service to the organisation
- Enlisting volunteers in training staff and other volunteers
- Involving volunteers in the annual planning process

Motivational orientation

In Chapter 2 we noted that people volunteer for a variety of different reasons. Sometimes psychologists categorise those motivations into three major categories – the need for achievement, the need for affiliation and the need for power. For volunteers who seem to be more motivated by one of these than another, you can tailor the recognition to fit the motivational need.

Achievement-oriented volunteers

■ Ideal recognition for this type of volunteer is additional information or more challenging tasks, such as a book on the subject area of the organisation or ability to participate in advanced training sessions or work with more difficult clients

■ Work being recognised is best linked to a very specific accomplishment

■ Phrasing of recognition through 'Best', 'Most' awards

■ Recognition decision should include 'Checkpoints' or 'Records'

■ Awardee should be selected by respected co-workers or recognised experts

Affiliation-oriented volunteers

■ Recognition should be given at group events

■ Recognition should be given in the presence of peers, family or other bonded groupings

■ Recognition item or award should have a 'personal touch'

■ Recognition should be organisational in nature, given by the organisation, with symbols of the organisation attached

■ Recognition should be voted for or affirmed by peers

■ If primary affiliate bonding is with a client, not others in the organisation, then the client should take part in the recognition, through a personal note of thanks or as presenter of the award

Power-oriented volunteers

■ Key aspect of recognition is 'promotion', conveying greater access to authority or information or a more important title or position

■ Recognition item should convey status, such as a special parking space

■ Recognition should be a commendation from somebody important, either known in the community or from higher up in the organisation

■ Audience for the recognition should include more senior members of the organisation and the community

■ Recognition should be announced to the wider community, put in the newspaper, volunteer newsletter and website

■ Recognition decisions should be made or ratified by the organisation's leadership

Style of volunteering

Recognition might also vary depending on whether the person is a long-term volunteer or only with you for a short period:

Long-term volunteer

- Recognition with and by peer group of volunteers and staff
- Recognition items make use of group symbols (business cards, name badges or clothing such as hats, uniforms and shirts)
- Recognition entails greater power, involvement, information about the organisation – 'earned' status and preference
- Presenter of recognition is a person in authority from within the organisation
- Recognition is linked to success in furthering the mission of the organisation

There are strong resemblances between the long-term volunteer and the affiliation-oriented volunteer. This is because long-term volunteers commonly form strong affiliate bonds with the organisation and its cause and with volunteers and other co-workers.

Short-term volunteer

- Recognition is given in immediate work unit or social group
- Recognition is 'portable'; something the volunteers can take with them when they leave – a present, photograph or other memorabilia of experience, or training that may benefit them in another setting
- Recognition is provided via home or work – letter to employer, church or family
- Presenter is either the immediate supervisor of the volunteer or the client with whom a relationship has been formed

The short-term volunteer is interested in very different forms of recognition, primarily those not directly connected as much to the organisational structure as to what is accomplished through volunteering or what volunteering there might mean for the volunteer. Zappala et al (2001) commented:

> Recognition for individual volunteers is therefore less about awards for years of service (the 'gold watch' approach) and more about providing feedback to the individual about the outcomes achieved through their project-based volunteering.

Staff versus volunteer perceptions of recognition

Staff may have a different idea to that of volunteers of what might be the desired form of recognition. Propst and Bentley (2000) found the following patterns in a survey of outdoor recreation managers and citizen volunteers in outdoor recreation programmes:

Citizen expectations and manager perceptions of what citizens expect regarding their participation in outdoor recreation or resource management/planning

Expectation	Managers %	Citizens %
Thank you	12	8
Public recognition	81	8
Nothing	24	62
More access to managers	24	14
More influence over policy decisions	33	26
Enjoyment	5	0
Respect	0	3

Other considerations in volunteer recognition

You should note that an 'ideal' recognition system might require a mixture of procedures in order to have something for every type of volunteer. This is not unusual and is quite appropriate. Heidrich (1990) summed this up quite pithily: 'There is no single recognition event that will make everybody happy.'

Many organisations fail to do this, with interesting results. Consider, for example, an all-too-typical organisation that gives its volunteer awards only according to the amount of time donated, a 'longevity' prize. If you are a short-term volunteer how do you feel about this system? Or perhaps your busy schedule limits the time you can offer? Could you possibly ever 'win' under these rules? What would this type of award suggest to you about the value that the organisation places upon your own contribution of time?

Mary Merrill (2002) commented on this phenomenon:

Many organizations over the years gradually fall into the pattern of recognizing longevity. They have volunteers that stay with them over the years and they look for new/different ways to recognize their ongoing commitment and loyalty.

Today's new volunteers are not always impressed with the 'tenure' badges. A large proportion of contemporary volunteers are looking for episodic, short-term, time-specific volunteer assignments. They are seeking ways to fit volunteering into an already busy work and/or family schedule. The last thing many of these new volunteers are interested in is a recognition system that focuses on length of service.

Michael (1990) noted an interesting example of the implications of this attitude among school volunteers:

> However, the committee heard from a number of volunteers, particularly corporate volunteers and professionals providing specialized services, that they would prefer recognition in the form of information from the schools about whether and how their volunteering makes a difference to students, specifically youngsters they have been tutoring and mentoring. In one case, volunteers declined to attend a recognition event that conflicted with their regularly scheduled activities with students.

You may also find differences based on how most volunteers go about their volunteering. One study, for example, found that volunteers who tend to work closely with other volunteers throughout the year tend not to be excited by the annual volunteer recognition lunch – yet another opportunity to get together with other volunteers whom they already see on a regular basis. Those volunteers who worked mostly in the community, with little contact with other volunteers, relished the idea of an annual gathering.

In a US survey of 4-H volunteers (whose programme is involved with serving and involving young people in rural communities through events and competitions), Culp and Schwartz (1998) found that volunteers considered these the most meaningful forms of recognition (in order of preference):

1 Thank-you notes
2 'Pat on the back'
3 Formal recognition banquets
4 Informal recognition (at a meeting)
5 Receiving plaques, pin-badges, trays, and such like
6 Phone calls
7 Recognition at a large regional event
8 Home visits

And volunteers ranked as the most meaningful source of the recognition:

1 4-H members
2 4-H club
3 County/community
4 4-H organisational staff
5 Other volunteers in the organisation
6 County-wide
7 District-wide
8 News media

A volunteer's cultural origin may make a difference to the type of desired recognition. Hobbs (2000) commented:

> Like other aspects of the volunteering process, recognition of contributions must be designed within the cultural context. In general, because Latinos are modest people, recognition is best carried out in ways where attention to the individual in front of large groups is minimized. Don't expect your Latino volunteers to attend a formal, community-wide recognition event. They will not attend recognition dinners; they will not find appearing before a meeting of county commissioners reinforcing.

Recognition processes can also be tailored by selecting the person who gives the recognition. The Buddhist Compassion Relief Tzu Chi Foundation, for example, has the following system for awarding of pin-badges honouring volunteer hours at different levels:

1 The Red pin should be presented by Department head.
2 The Orange, Yellow, Green, Blue, Purple Blue and Purple Pin will be presented by Chief Executive Officer of the Buddhist Compassion Relief Tzu Chi Foundation, USA (Mr Stephen Huang at special ceremonies).
3 The Gold Pin will be presented by Master Cheng Yen.

Recognition provided by top management can send a compelling signal about the organisation valuing volunteer service, especially if it is given in an informal way. Kuyper (1993) wrote about one example of this:

> One museum director circulates through the museum once a day to thank volunteers who are on duty. Such efforts on the part of museum administration go a long way toward helping volunteers feel satisfied and rewarded.

Training can also be a means of providing recognition, with the volunteer qualifying to attend either in-service or external training. One organisation in the US that uses volunteer drivers honours a select few each year by sending them on a defensive driving course. This not only upgrades the skills of the volunteers in respect of their volunteer duties but also allows them to qualify for lower rates on their personal vehicle insurance.

Local organisations should strive to make recognition given to volunteers known in the community, not just within the organisation. Ogilvie (2004) commented on the results of this for volunteers at a homeless shelter in New York City:

> In the neighborhood settings like Sacred Heart, the respect that an outstanding volunteer is given by his or her peers knows no bounds and it

is as likely to be accorded at the grocery store as in the shelter. This makes these intangible rewards and punishments more potent motivators of desired actions, which is one of the reasons why it is easier to develop community with propinquity.

In and of itself, recognition is not likely to be the determinative factor in any volunteer's decision to continue with an organisation. Recognition, however, does tend to have an impact when taken into consideration with other factors. Fahey and Walker (2001) commented that:

> Whilst respect and recognition are not strong motivators in themselves, lack of them affects retention. Individuals indicated that whilst they don't look for recognition, lack of it can make them feel very negative when they feel down. These sentiments were expressed more strongly by longer serving members and it seems that lack of appreciation by the organisation and community could tip the scales in an individual's decision to leave.

Not mentioned on any of the above surveys but generally recognised as highly effective by most volunteer managers is the practice of providing food as a recognition technique. The Burning Man Volunteer Management Team noted in its Afterburn Report 2002 (http://afterburn.burningman.com/02/community/volunteer.html):

> The Volunteer Team arranged assorted events during the year to thank our local volunteers. We held our first volunteer barbecue in Golden Gate Park. This well-attended event was marked by a special Bubble Show at the end! We organized the Town Hall Volunteer Recruitment Meeting at SOMArts, which also included a barbecue that attracted hundreds of prospective volunteers looking for ways to support the organization.

The relationship between recognition and feeling involved

Frequently, volunteer recognition involves the giving of some kind of physical token of appreciation – a certificate, flowers, a gift certificate or a card. By giving volunteers the right kind of tokens, we can help them to feel unique and connected at the same time.

The previous chapter covered some of the things that paid staff have that volunteers do not, such as e-mail addresses, name badges, business cards and opportunities for training and, indeed, this is a real concern. If volunteers are not likely to stay for very long, it would be a waste of a charity's precious, limited resources to have business cards printed for them.

One way to solve this dilemma is to give these items to volunteers as recognition for their contributions to the charity. While we are ordinarily not big fans of giving volunteers recognition simply for turning up, giving these identifying items as recognition for hours of service can make volunteers feel connected to the organisation and, because they are awarded for longevity, other staff might feel that it is less likely to be an expense wasted on someone who might not turn up the next day. After 50 hours, for example, a volunteer might be given a name badge like the ones that staff wear. After 100 hours of service they might have an e-mail address and so forth. When volunteers demonstrate their staying power, the organisation may be more likely to make the investment in these costly items. That in turn produces more staying power.

Creating mutual understanding

When people in a diverse group are able to accept each other's uniqueness, the motivational climate is greatly improved. But there is an even greater benefit to the charity; the capacity of the group is also greatly strengthened.

People's unique personalities result from the fact that we each have a unique history. This history, our experience, leads to unique perspectives. One of the keys to leading an effective group is to realise that differences in perspective are a sign of strength and not a weakness.

There is an old story about blindfolded people who each touch a different part of an elephant. They then have a conversation about what elephants are like. The belief of one, based on the experience of touching the tusk, is that an elephant is cylindrical, hard and has a pointed end. Another hears this assertion and cannot believe how wrong that person has got it, insisting that, while cylindrical, the elephant is flexible and has intermittent hot air puffs coming out of the end. A third, whose experience involved feeling the ear, tells the others that they are both idiots, that an elephant is a flat, flexible sheet.

People who disagree are not unlike those blindfolded people. They have adopted beliefs based on their own life experiences. To the degree that those experiences are different, we will therefore develop different beliefs. Like the blindfolded people, we believe the others to be wrong. In fact, we tend to think they are ignorant and in need of education because our position is so obviously right.

In order for individuals in a group to feel both unique and connected, each group member must realise that a person can have a different opinion without being wrong. They must realise that the differences make the group stronger, not weaker. If we all had a common background, if we all touched the tail of the elephant, we would quickly come to an agreement about the nature of the elephant and make quick decisions based on our common beliefs. However, our decisions would not be as good as if we had listened to and accepted as truth the opinions of those who had different experiences.

The relationship between uniqueness and teams

When people feel safe to be themselves in a group, when they know the group will accept and value them as members even when they make statements that are contrary to the beliefs or values of others, they are able to feel unique and connected at the same time. To fulfil the promise of a diverse team, each member must have the capacity to understand the others. This is much harder to achieve than it sounds, and it does not often happen without work.

If two volunteers, or a volunteer and a member of staff, seem to see the world very differently, you might ask them if they would be willing to participate in a discussion in an attempt to increase their understanding of each other's points of view. Pick one to express a point of view first and give the other the challenge of summarising that point of view to the satisfaction of the first person. Both will be surprised at how difficult this can be. If they persevere, both will gain an understanding of the other's unique perspective and perhaps some of the reasons for it. The usual result of this exercise is that conflict between the two parties is greatly reduced and the wisdom of each is greatly expanded. And because they now see the tusk as well as the trunk, they have a greater appreciation for the whole elephant.

Final thoughts on volunteer recognition

Volunteer programme managers have a tendency to think of volunteer recognition as something that is 'done' by the volunteer programme or the charity. In reality, a true feeling of recognition is much more complex, and is more dependent upon people's perception of the attitudes of those around them.

A study done in Vancouver by the Strategic Volunteering Advisory Group and Isabella Mori (2001) among volunteers at a low-income downtown shelter community illustrates this principle:

Volunteer co-ordinators discussed formal volunteer appreciation (dinners, outings, etc.) at some length. However, that was a topic that was not once mentioned by volunteers. When volunteers felt appreciated, they mostly mentioned day-to-day feedback on their work, as well as 'feeling like a staff member'. They also expressed not feeling appreciated, for example that their experience was not being taken seriously by staff ... for volunteers, day-to-day, on-the-spot appreciation and recognition is most important. That includes a feeling that they have a voice and are taken seriously. When volunteers feel – realistically or unrealistically – that this type of appreciation and recognition is not occurring throughout the year, they may see formal volunteer appreciation as something superficial or artificial.

What needs to be done is as little as watching out for work well done, for good team work, for a great attitude, and then commenting on it.

Vineyard (2001) summed this up neatly:

Recognition must be an attitude that permeates the entire planning and implementation efforts throughout the year. It is far more than pins, plaques and certificates ...

chapter (5)

CREATING MEANINGFUL VOLUNTEER EXPERIENCES

In addition to feelings of connection and uniqueness, people with high self-esteem feel a sense of power. When we talk about power in this context, we are not talking about power over others but rather what might be described as personal power. Personal power stems from a combination of feelings of effectiveness and control. This chapter examines how the volunteer experience can build this combination.

Volunteers gain a sense of effectiveness when they feel that their actions make a difference. Volunteer programmes produce this sense of effectiveness when:

- Volunteers see how their actions are related to the mission of the charity
- Volunteer positions are defined in terms of results
- Volunteers get feedback on how their actions are making a difference.

It is noted how these elements appear in Colomy et al (1987) results of a study of the factors in a volunteer position rated highly by volunteers (given in rank order of importance):

1. Helping others
2. Clearly defined responsibilities
3. Interesting work
4. Competence of immediate supervisor
5. Supervisor guidance
6. Seeing results of my work
7. Working with a respected community organization
8. Reasonable work schedule
9. Doing the thing I do best
10. Suitable workload
11. Freedom to decide how to get things done

Connecting volunteers to the mission

Charities exist to alleviate social problems of some kind or to meet the needs of a given population. Alleviating those problems or meeting those needs is the purpose or mission of charities. As shown in Chapter 2, when volunteers can see how their actions contribute to achieving the mission, they gain a great sense of purpose and effectiveness.

Scott and Caldwell (1996), in a study of hospice volunteers, found that over 96% listed 'believe in hospice mission' as a reason for continuing volunteering – far beyond 'opportunity for personal growth' (70%) and 'feel needed' (69%), the second and third highest responses.

Starnes and Wymer (1999), in another study, noted: 'People tend to continue as hospice volunteers when they strongly believe in the mission and feel that their work in support of the mission is valued.'

In Ireland, the National Committee on Volunteering (2002) found that:

> Both women and men volunteered because of believing in the cause, and for men this was slightly more important than for women ... Belief in the cause increased in importance as women became older and was most significant for the group of women most likely to volunteer, that is those in their 40s and 50s. By contrast belief in the cause was most important for men aged under 30 who were among those least likely to volunteer.

Belief in the mission of the organisation is one of the strongest ways to generate retention – it indicates that the volunteer has internalised the importance of participation, and this internalised belief will encourage them to continue volunteering.

To connect volunteer roles to the mission in this way, begin by defining the mission in terms of a solution to a community problem or the meeting of a community need. When you talk to volunteers about their tasks, talk about their contribution to the mission.

This is easy to do when the volunteers are involved in direct client service. If the mission is that everyone be functionally literate, for example, those volunteers who are involved in tutoring clients are obviously making a contribution to that end. When volunteers are involved in support activities, such as posting fundraising letters or filing documents, the connection is less obvious. By letting such volunteers know how their activities have helped the agency to achieve its mission, however, you give their activities extra meaning.

In addition to thanking a volunteer for their office assistance, for example, you could say something like 'Because you came in today, we were able to free our staff to do four extra hours of teaching clients to read.' Alternatively, you could say something like 'The fundraising letter you sent out raised £600. This enables us to provide tutoring to an additional student.' Such statements help volunteers see the connection to the mission of the agency and to feel that their actions have additional meaning.

Hashim (2003) noted the power and ease of this technique:

> For many volunteers, there is no better form of recognition than to know how their work has contributed to the cause. This can be done by sharing the outcome of a project with volunteers, such as how much money was raised from an event and how that money is going to help people with hemophilia. It could mean sharing the story of a child who participated in a summer camp, and how the experience affected him.

Elliston (2002) noted what happens in the absence of this belief: 'Those who don't see the connection of task to mission will feel that their efforts are wasted and leave.'

Volunteers can also develop a sense of shared pride in contributing to the mission by writing newsletter articles about their experiences. The newsletter of one charity features articles written by volunteers on the subject of what makes them proud to be part of the organisation. When other volunteers read these articles, it reminds them of why they are proud to be involved. These feelings of pride translate into feelings of having been a part of accomplishing the mission of the organisation.

Designing volunteer positions for results

We can also enhance a volunteer's sense of effectiveness by holding volunteers responsible for achieving results, rather than simply for performing a set of activities or 'job duties'. If they are responsible for results or outcomes, they are focused on the end product of what they do and they get the satisfaction of making progress towards a meaningful accomplishment. If, on the other hand, they are responsible only for the activities that may lead to some undefined result, they are divorced from that satisfaction. Crime prevention volunteers in a Neighbourhood Watch programme, for example, gain far more satisfaction if they are given the responsibility for reducing burglaries, and their effectiveness is measured against this yardstick (insofar as is possible), than if they see the position as the activity of knocking on doors to talk to people about planting 'hostile shrubbery' under their windows.

Most job descriptions for volunteers or for paid staff are not defined in terms of results. Instead, they merely list a series of activities that are supposed to be performed. The result is never mentioned. In most cases, the responsibility for the result is fragmented; with several people each having a few activities to perform if the result is to be achieved. In fact, the responsibility is sometimes so fragmented that the volunteer loses sight of the result. As a direct consequence of this, results are poorly and inefficiently obtained and the volunteer gets bored.

Grossman and Furano (2002) noted:

> Having well-defined tasks laid out and communicated to the volunteer (and to those with whom the volunteer will work) is the first step in attracting and retaining effective volunteers. Ill-defined tasks, like 'Help the teacher', communicate to both the volunteer and the teacher that their work really is not critical. Volunteer jobs should be carefully designed to provide the volunteer with meaningful work in which both he or she and paid staff who may work beside them know how the volunteer's contributions help to achieve the mission of the organization.

Clark and Shimoni (2002b) added:

> One of the challenges of keeping volunteers engaged over the long term is demonstrating measurable outcomes. Volunteers and others want and need to see benchmarks or milestones of accomplishment to know that an initiative is moving forward. Those milestones need to be clearly articulated or demonstrated. While the vision of the initiative may be very long-term, volunteers need to see progress towards that vision within their term of service.

With some volunteer positions, results can be obvious, as Thompson and Bono (1993) noted:

> When called to respond to a fire, medical, or rescue emergency, volunteer firefighters participate in an activity which has a real, important, and immediately tangible outcome. They understand that their intervention has the capacity to defeat grave threats to life and property, imbuing these firefighters with a true sense of empowerment.

With other volunteer positions, seeing results can be more difficult.

Because it can be difficult at first to grasp the concept of defining positions in terms of results, we shall look at some examples. Volunteers in a drug misuse programme, for example, may be told that their role is to spend three hours a week counselling a client. This is a statement of an activity to be performed. No result of the counselling has been specified, and if the volunteer does not achieve much, we should not be surprised. The work as defined requires no particular skill, other than sitting in a room with someone for three hours. To define the result, we need to ask, 'What is the outcome we want from the counselling? What do we want the volunteer to accomplish in these three hours per week?' The answer would probably be something like 'Clients will be able to cope with daily life without resorting to the use of drugs.' By defining this desired result for each volunteer counsellor, we offer a challenging and worthwhile accomplishment for the volunteer to be working towards.

Similarly, volunteers in a school programme might be told that their role is to work with children on reading skills. When we ask only that someone 'work with' the children, we are not creating any responsibility for helping the children to learn. There is no challenge in the position when it is defined in this way. It is better to specify the specific skill improvements that the volunteer is responsible for helping the child to achieve. The result might read something like 'Bring the child's reading abilities up to grade six reading level.'

Hands for Nature (2002), a community greening coalition in Ontario, suggested the following:

> Because volunteers are motivated by their commitment to improve the environment, support their motivation and interest by keeping them posted on any progress resulting from their work. This can be as simple as short e-mail updates to your volunteer roster, posting updates on your website and through your group's newsletter, annual report or any other communication materials. If you have the time and resources, other more innovative and interactive tools can be used to let people know the difference they have made – such as site tours.

When we define volunteer assignments in terms of results, we help meet people's need for a sense of achievement or accomplishment. It helps them to feel that their volunteer activity is valuable and worthwhile. It also helps the volunteer programme to operate more effectively. When people know what they are supposed to accomplish, they are more likely to do so. If we want to achieve meaningful results through our volunteers, it makes sense that we should let them know what results we expect and then hold the volunteers responsible for accomplishing them.

As Gidron (1984) noted following a study of sources of work satisfaction among volunteers:

> ... in order to be satisfied, a volunteer needs, above all, a task in which self-expression is possible – a task which gives the volunteer the opportunity to develop abilities and skills, a task which is seen as a challenge, a task where achievements can be seen.

Giving feedback on effectiveness

We can further enhance volunteers' sense of effectiveness by giving them information as to whether and to what degree the results are being achieved. If we do not do this, the statement of result will fail to have any motivating value and it will be impossible for both volunteer and supervisor to know how well the volunteer is doing.

Many volunteer programme managers shy away from measuring volunteer performance, thinking that doing so would discourage or demotivate them. The opposite is more likely to be the case. If people are unable to tell either how well they are doing or whether they are succeeding or failing, they tend to become bored with the activity. There is also no incentive to try a different course of action if you do not know that your present course is not working.

Most volunteer programmes probably do little to evaluate the performance of their volunteers. Wandersman and Alderman (1993) found that only 33% of the chapters (branches) of the American Cancer Society (ACS) performed an evaluation of their volunteers, and ACS is one of the better organised national health volunteer systems.

For some positions the measure of performance is fairly obvious and easy to state. In the case of crime prevention volunteers, for example, the number of burglaries in their area is a readily available statistical measure. We can use these statistics (providing the volunteers are responsible for the same geographical area for which statistics are being compiled) to measure the result of keeping people safe from burglaries. Every time a burglary occurs in their area, they will naturally ask 'what could have been done to prevent that?' These thoughts spur their creativity and encourage new, even more effective, approaches. If the assignment is merely defined as engraving personal identification numbers onto people's stereos, however, and there is no feedback to the volunteers as to how well they are doing, there will be little likelihood that more effective approaches will be tried.

In other cases, we find the measure more difficult. In the case of the Girl Guide leader whose result is to help her girls develop self-assurance, we need to do some hard work to decide how we are going to measure progress. We need to ask questions such as 'How will we know if girls gain self-assurance? What would we see when they are and when they aren't self-assured? What questions could we ask them to determine their degree of self-confidence?' We would then work out how to collect these data and feed them back to the volunteer so she can tell how effective her actions are.

Many volunteer programme managers do not want to do this much work, so they take the easy course of holding the volunteers accountable only for performing a set of activities or spending a certain number of hours in the service of the charity. By doing so, however, they deprive the volunteers of the ability to tell how well they are doing. They also deprive them of a sense of accomplishment.

Taking the time necessary to define how to measure volunteer progress towards results is management work. It is an essential job that all managers should engage in but many do not. In not doing so, they throw away a major motivator.

Many volunteer programme managers who do measure performance tend to measure the wrong things. They keep track of things such as hours spent, miles driven or client contacts made. These measures tend to lack any real meaning because they do not tell us whether the volunteer is accomplishing anything of value. They do not measure whether the desired result is being achieved.

To determine how to measure a given result, involve the volunteers who do the work. Ask them these two questions:

- 'What information would tell us if you are successfully achieving the result?'
- 'How could we collect it?'

As in the examples above, these two questions will tell you what information needs to be gathered and fed back to the volunteers.

Providing this information on success can be critical to the retention of volunteers. Fischer and Shaffer (1993) noted:

> If volunteers perceive their work as successful, they will feel competent, and if they feel competent, they will make further commitment of their time.

Measuring performance makes it possible to introduce an element of challenge. People are challenged when they are trying to reach a target.

When we measure people's performance in this way, we also make possible the setting of records. Records are tremendously motivating. People do ridiculous things daily, such as making an omelette that weighs four tons, in order to break records. The *Guinness Book of Records* lists some of these frivolous achievements. If people spend time and effort doing such silly things voluntarily, think of the productive work they might do if there were records to set for something more serious!

Some volunteer roles may be difficult to produce measures for because the results take a long time to occur. Clark and Shimoni (2002b) commented: '... in long-term social change initiatives, change often takes many years to become apparent. Volunteers involved in such initiatives may express frustration at not being able to see the differences they are making.'

They recommended a number of ways to compensate for this:

- Clarify the nature of the social change sought so as to give volunteers a common vision of the long-term goal.
- Develop clear short-term goals or milestones so that volunteers can see the progress they are making.
- Communicate accomplishments widely so that volunteers' contributions can be recognized by the larger community.

Providing a sense of control to volunteers

Our sense of personal power comes not only from a sense that our actions are effective but also from a sense that we decide what actions we will take. People with a sense of personal power feel that they are masters of their fate rather than helpless victims of circumstance. They feel they can decide to do something about the problems they see and that when they take those actions, those actions will make a difference.

When we talk about giving volunteers a sense of control, we are talking about giving them the authority to think, the authority to plan and evaluate their work, and the authority to decide what to do. Volunteers have a degree of autonomy in determining what they do and how they go about doing it. With this authority the individual or team of volunteers not only does the work but can also play some part in deciding how to do it.

Many volunteer programme managers have a built-in resistance to allowing volunteers this authority. For one thing, the volunteer may work only a few hours a month and so have difficulty keeping up with what is going on. On the other hand, standard management practice holds that it is the supervisor's job to do the planning and make decisions, and the employee's job to carry out whatever the supervisor thinks should be done.

Indeed, when a volunteer first comes on board, this may be the most comfortable way to proceed. As volunteers learn the job and begin to work out what is going on, however, the fact that they are only doing what someone else decides begins to sap their motivation and dilute their feelings of pride in what they accomplish. They will tend either to resent being told what to do or to lose interest in the job. Either of these will increase the likelihood of their dropping out.

This does not mean that we should abdicate our responsibility for ensuring good results from volunteers. Obviously, we cannot afford to have all our volunteers doing whatever they think is best, with no guidance. We need to make sure that they are all working towards the achievement of a coordinated and agreed set of goals. What we can do, however, is involve them in the planning and decision-making process so that they feel a sense of authority over the 'how' of their job. We should ask: 'How would a person who tells the volunteers what to do know what to tell them?'

Alternatively, we could ask: 'What does the volunteer's supervisor do in order to work out what to tell the volunteer to do?'

We can then include those thinking tasks in the volunteer's job description, healing the schism between thinking and doing. In a sense, in doing this we give volunteers back their brains.

By 'empowering' volunteers, we mean making them more autonomous, more capable of independent action. The wisdom of this approach is that it is easier to get good results from empowered people than from people who are dependent. We can do this by giving them authority to decide, within limits, how they will go about achieving the results for which they are responsible. In such a relationship the manager becomes a source of help for the volunteer rather than being pushy or controlling. This not only feels better for the volunteer but allows the manager to spend less time making decisions about the volunteer's work and instead allows more time to think strategically and to concentrate on grasping the opportunities that will never be seen if they are submerged in the day-to-day detail. It also gives more time to work with other staff of the agency on how to improve their involvement of volunteers.

As an example of providing volunteers with their own sense of control and autonomy, consider the following from a study of the Travelers Aid Society (TAS) volunteer programme in America. McComb (1995) in a study of the TAS programme at Washington Reagan National Airport noted the following ('Martha' is the TAS volunteer programme manager, an old friend of the authors):

> Connected to the rewards of competence and excelling was the reward of autonomy. Martha told me that she wanted volunteers to feel that what they thought or did mattered, and was careful to give them ownership of their environment. Volunteers did not explicitly mention autonomy as a reward, yet autonomy was apparent to me. I understood that Martha's motto of 'there's policy and then there's style' meant that different ways of doing the job were permissible. And volunteers did have ownership of the desk on their shifts. For instance, one volunteer decided on his own that the desks needed 'Information' signs as well as Travelers Aid signs. He went ahead and had signs professionally printed for each desk; TAS reimbursed his costs.

The result of this approach, along with the other practices discussed, is significant: 'TAS volunteers stay. Eight had worked for 15 to 20 years, nine for 10 to 14 years, working 52 three- or four-and-a-half-hour shifts a week.'

Colomy et al (1987), in a study of volunteers at various agencies, perhaps summarised this whole chapter when they cited the importance that volunteers give to what they refer to as 'situational facilities', a variety of job-related factors including suitable workload, clearly defined responsibilities, competence of their supervisor and a reasonable work schedule. They concluded:

> Perhaps the single most important finding reported in this study is the relatively high importance volunteers accord situational facilities. The high ranking and high mean score of situational facilities are evident both for the sample as a whole and for each of the three sub-groups of volunteers. In addition to the intrinsic and extrinsic incentives associated with volunteer work, then, it appears that individuals strongly desire conditions and organizational settings that facilitate effective and efficient volunteer work.

Don't we all?

chapter ⑥

INSTILLING ORGANISATIONAL VALUES IN VOLUNTEERS

Underlying the purpose of the effective organisation is a set of values. Much has been written about the importance of organisational values to a group's success. An effective group must have a single set of values; otherwise members will be likely to wind up working at cross-purposes with interpersonal conflict being the order of the day. When volunteers work in a place that is riven with conflict they will find the experience unpleasant and they will do something else with their time.

McSweeney and Alexander (1996) noted the importance of clearly defined values:

> Values are the set of beliefs the organisation holds dear. They may cover the way in which you work, the context in which you try to achieve your purpose and the outcomes you hope for. Talking about values helps to clarify for those who work for you the expectations you have of them.

Values are also related to self-esteem. People with high self-esteem have some clear mental models of how to behave. In an organisational context, those mental models are the charity's values.

When we talk about values, we are talking about a set of principles that guide people's behaviour. We mean a sense of what is right and wrong. Examples of organisational values include the promise of help to the client at all costs, taking the initiative, accepting responsibility, win-win thinking and innovation.

Here are some of the core values that drive the Boys and Girls Clubs of Canada:

- We care about children and youth.
- We acknowledge that a sense of self worth is fundamental to individual dignity.
- We understand children and youth need to be heard.
- We believe a sense of belonging is essential to healthy growth.
- We foster cultural understanding and acceptance.
- We are committed to volunteerism.
- We value and practice cooperative approaches.

Having identified these core principles, the national organisation then expects the local boys and girls club volunteers, and staff, to act in accordance with those values. By giving their people a clear sense of what is right and wrong, managers are more comfortable with their people making decisions. If the club were approached by the Boy Scouts with the idea of putting on a training course for youth on self-image, for example, the decision would be guided by the principle, 'We value and practice cooperative approaches.' If a volunteer sees two children engaged in taunting each other with ethnic slurs, his response would be guided by the value, 'We foster cultural understanding and acceptance.' Also, if potential volunteers needed to have the club open at different hours in order to do their work, the decision would be guided by the principle, 'We are committed to volunteerism.'

The Gay and Lesbian Rights Lobby of Australia enunciated this concept in its Code of Conduct (www.glrl.org.au/OLD/html/Code_of_Conduct.htm), after listing its organisational values (equality, social justice, fairness, accountability, openness/transparency):

> These values are at the heart of our mission and our existence as a community organisation. They therefore form a basis for this code of conduct.

> In developing a Code of Conduct it is not possible to specifically cover every situation that could arise and raise an ethical issue. When dealing with situations that are not covered, we should seek to advance the interests of the organisation and act in accordance with its values and mission.

Clear values are essential to volunteer empowerment. Internalised values enable the manager to empower the volunteer to make decisions and maintain some assurance that the volunteer will decide to do the right thing.

Most organisations do not have clear values of this sort. If the values are not clear, volunteers will not be sure of the best course of action. When they are unsure, they are likely to ask their supervisor what to do, diverting staff attention from other matters. When the values are unclear, therefore, volunteers consume more management time.

All of this means that the manager who wants to build a truly outstanding organisation needs to go beyond the important questions of 'What are we trying to achieve?' and 'How will we achieve it?' to 'Who are we? What do we stand for? What do we believe in? What are the characteristics of our organisation? What does it mean to be one of us? What kind of person is lucky enough to work here?' These questions ought to be considered frequently by every leader, and the positive answers to these questions ought to be broadcast frequently to the staff and volunteers to help create a strong sense of the group's standards and traits.

As Nelson et al noted in 1995:

> Because organizational commitment is based on volunteer attachment to organizational ideals, a volunteer program manager must take great care to communicate the organization's philosophy. It is the essential inspiring vision that binds the program's character, social role, goals and objectives to the volunteer's self-image.

Establishing statements of values

Essentially, the values of a charity should be based on the promise it is trying to keep to the people it serves. In order to establish organisational values, begin with the mission statement. Ask yourself 'What is the promise that this mission statement implies that we are trying to keep? What is the promise that underlies our reason for existence?' A child abuse agency, for example, had as its mission that every child should be free from abuse. Its answer to the question, 'What is the promise you are trying to keep?' is 'A safe and stable home for every child.' This guides the behaviour of its volunteers and staff. As the agency makes decisions about what information to seek in advocating for the rights of a child, who to talk to, and what to recommend to juvenile authorities, it is guided by this promise.

Once the promise has been defined, the next questions are:

■ What principles should guide our behaviour as we attempt to keep this promise?
■ What principles should guide us as we interact with each other and with our clients?
■ What principles should guide our managers' interactions with their people?

The answers to these questions might include words such as 'integrity', 'mutual respect' and 'empowerment'. They might also include phrases such as 'We put the client's welfare above our own', or 'We practise non-judgemental listening.' Moscow Charity House, for example, identified the following values to guide the behaviour of the volunteers who distribute clothing and other items to low-income pensioners:

- honesty
- openness
- social partnership
- voluntary action

- respect for all people
- altruism.

The British Red Cross operates under seven fundamental principles:

- humanity
- impartiality
- neutrality
- independence
- voluntary service
- unity
- universality.

Each organisation or cause needs to find its own unique way to describe what it believes in and what will govern its conduct. The more these beliefs are discussed and internalised by staff and volunteers, the more likely that behaviour will conform to organisational values. As an example of working to develop this consensus on organisational values the British evangelical Christian charity, Tearfund, puts its 'Basis of Faith' on information brochures that describe individual volunteer positions. Adherence to the religious beliefs in the Basis of Faith is as important a qualification as the skills needed to fulfil the position.

What does that mean we do?

The difference between values and slogans is that values guide the action of each group member. Values need to be internalised by everyone. When the line between what is right and what is wrong is clear, group members know when they are stepping over the line and are more likely to refrain from doing so. It is also easier to bring someone who is behaving inappropriately back in line when the line itself is clear and when the value is clear.

In a value-driven organisation, people have a clear vision of what its principles mean they are supposed to do. Too often, top management develops statements of principles, announces them and then assumes that members of the organisation will follow them. Because there is often a lack of communication between top management and those doing the bulk of the work of the organisation, these assumptions tend to go unchecked. As a consequence, there can be a great difference between what management assumes is happening and what is really happening.

A volunteer fire department, for example, developed a series of five values, one of which was 'We care about the citizens of our community.' This was a sentiment that was hard to argue with, but it was vague to the members of the department. To make this come alive, the chief met with the volunteers one night after drill and asked, 'What does this mean we do in the event of a fire?'

The first answer from the group was 'We get to the scene as fast as we can and put out the fire as quickly as possible.' This was something they already did, so the chief went on probing, asking them about how the principle would apply in various specific situations. One of these was 'What if the householders were present while we were fighting the fire?' After some discussion, firefighters realised it was important to keep them informed of what they were doing as they fought the fire instead of ignoring them or treating them as obstacles. Similarly, the group decided that if there were a child present at the scene, they should try to offer comfort. As a consequence, they began to carry teddy bears on the fire engines.

After this and several similar meetings, the firefighters had a clear idea of what the values statements meant. They became a guide to their decision-making on the job.

Occasionally values will conflict, forcing an organisation to decide which of the values should take priority. Miller et al (2002) reported on a situation in which a museum that prided itself on efficiency decided to involve disabled volunteers, thus fostering the value of inclusiveness:

> For a few of the nondisabled volunteers, productivity occasionally took priority over involving their peers with disabilities and socialization. Two types of situations appeared to instigate such behavior – when museum staff became highly involved (hands on) in the task at hand and appeared to communicate a need for increased productivity in order to complete it within a set duration of time, or when the volunteers with disabilities arrived late to the volunteer site and nondisabled peers began working without them. On these occasions, several nondisabled volunteers appeared to be already set in a productivity mode that they struggled to break when the volunteers with disabilities arrived and attempted to join them.

Making values about volunteer involvement a reality

Many charities would, if asked, espouse support for the organisational value of involving volunteers. The British Red Cross, for example, says:

We have a long history of volunteering which we are committed to maintaining because:

- service participants place special value on the care which skilled and trained volunteers can give – care given willingly, in their own time, without expectation of material reward
- volunteers enable us to draw on a very wide pool of skill, derived from professional and personal experience, which enriches the services we offer
- volunteers provide an invaluable insight to the needs of the communities in which they live, thus better informing our work.

Making this value a reality, however, is a very different proposition.

Consider the value statement of Community Service Volunteers (CSV), one of the largest volunteer-involving organisations in the UK:

We believe:

- Everyone has something significant to offer the community. We therefore actively encourage diversity and reject no one.
- Public and non-profit organisations and the community thrive on the contribution of volunteers.
- Access to training and lifelong learning is essential to personal development and community strength.

Note the phrase 'reject no one' in the first value statement. CSV takes this statement seriously and expends considerable effort and ingenuity in volunteer interviews making the ability of everyone to volunteer with a CSV programme a reality. It requires creativity in design of volunteer positions and, occasionally, the willingness to provide additional management resources. However, as an organisation that truly believes that volunteering is something which should be encouraged and enabled, both for the good of organisations and of the larger community, CSV fosters the extra effort to make its value a matter of practice.

One way to connect the organisational value to what it should do in actually supporting volunteers is to develop a statement of commitment giving further guidance. The following is an example of such a statement, developed by the Alberta Children's Hospital (ACH) in Canada:

Statement of commitment to the volunteer

The Alberta Children's Hospital [ACH] recognizes the contribution of volunteers in assisting staff to fulfill the mission of the hospital.

Towards the continued pursuit of excellence in volunteerism and in support of volunteers as valued members of the ACH team, the hospital's administration makes the following commitment to the volunteer community at ACH:

1   The hospital will support a Volunteer Resources Department providing appropriate staffing to manage the volunteer program.

2   Hospital staff, both professional and support, who are directing volunteers will be oriented to the needs of volunteers. In specific terms, all new staff, as part of their orientation, will receive instruction from Volunteer Resources. All staff working with volunteers will receive ongoing education from Volunteer Resources as required.

3   Hospital staff will play a role in the orientation, directing, evaluation and recognition on volunteers working in their areas.

4   Staff will facilitate a positive environment for volunteers working in their areas. This will involve welcoming them, assisting them, mentoring them when necessary and thanking them regularly for their contributions.

5   Staff working with volunteers will be recognized for this contribution.

Signed in March 1998 by the Administrative Leaders of the Alberta Children's Hospital and the Regional Senior Operating Officers responsible for the hospital and its volunteer program.

Involving others in communicating values

Although the primary responsibility for establishing shared values is that of the leader, it is best to involve as many people as possible in delineating what these values are. Using questions such as those in the previous example, the leader should guide the group in a discussion of what principles the group believes should guide its actions.

Do not let the list of values get too long. Group those that are similar into broader categories. For example, if the group comes up with characteristics such as 'caring', 'concerned' and 'dedicated to clients', you might group them into the larger category of being service-oriented. You do not want your volunteers having to try to remember 16 principles to apply in order to make a decision.

Once these broader values have been developed, ask the group to make a commitment to them as guiding principles. Ask 'Are you willing to help build an organisation that lives according to these values? Are you willing to create an excellent organisation based on these criteria?'

Although it is unlikely that anyone would say 'no' to such a question, some might come up with barriers that make it difficult to live up to the values. If the group decides, for example, that it is important to project a positive, caring attitude towards clients, someone might point out that the burdensome, bureaucratic procedures of the organisation make service slow and inconvenient for clients. Someone might say something like 'It is difficult to project a caring attitude when people are frustrated by filling out the same information on 12 different forms in four different locations.' Leaders welcome such objections because they point out areas in which the system can be improved. Once people see that positive changes are being made to help make the values a reality, their enthusiasm will increase. People get excited about being part of an excellent organisation.

The differences between values and procedures

When charities do not take the time to do the work described above, situations inevitably arise whereby there is confusion about the right thing to do. In the face of this, the typical organisation responds by establishing a standard operating procedure. In time this produces a manual of regulations too comprehensive to be read or understood by anyone and too rigid if enforced to allow creativity or application to new situations. Volunteers and paid staff find this a depressing prospect.

As Ilsley (1990) commented:

> Volunteers who feel they are helpless to follow their own interests, constantly enmeshed in nets of seemingly meaningless rules, are not likely to remain with an organization for long.

National organisations with local volunteer units are particularly good at creating very large manuals of procedures, policies, rules and supportive material, much of which is posted out to local volunteer officers. Most of it is never read, although much of it is religiously passed from volunteer leader to volunteer leader and then stored in the garage.

The relationship between uniqueness and values

Earlier we stressed the need for volunteers to feel free to be themselves and to disclose, through their behaviour, who they truly are. On rare occasions, this can lead to difficulties in adhering to the organisation's values. Imagine an organisation that places a high value on service to others, on putting the client first. Imagine that it involves a volunteer who places a high value on being assertive with others. Imagine that that volunteer encounters a frustrated client. The client vents his frustration with the organisation by raising his voice, or even calling the volunteer a name. The volunteer, acting according to her own unique values, raises her voice in turn, saying, 'Don't take that tone with me.' This leads to an escalation of the client's frustration. How does a charity respond to such a situation in a way that honours the volunteer's unique personality and also remains true to its values?

There are at least two ways to do this: one easy and the other difficult. The easy approach is to put volunteers in positions where they are unlikely to encounter this conflict, positions not involved in direct client service or public contact, for example.

The more effective, but more time-consuming approach is to train volunteers to handle the situation in a way in which they honour their own principles while providing empathetic service to the client. The charity might train or coach volunteers in how to defuse an angry client, how to ask questions instead of becoming defensive and how to understand the client's frustration to the point where they can put themselves in the client's shoes.

There are, of course, situations in which the value conflict is so great that the charity might find it best to part ways with the volunteer. A volunteer with a sexist or homophobic set of values working in a charity which values everyone's equality, for example, may just be inappropriate for the charity. By defining the charity's values, such inappropriateness becomes obvious to both parties and the parting will be easier.

Despite the importance of clear values, most voluntary organisations do not do a good job of either establishing or making values clear and real. The National Committee on Volunteering reports (2002) that among Irish charities:

> There was no evidence of familiarity with the language or concepts to articulate their organisation's values or ethos ... In a single organisation there could be 10 or 15 descriptions of the organisation, of which two, perhaps [were] connected to formal core values as declared by the organisations ... For volunteers, the core values are one level and they [the volunteers] are positioned at another.

chapter (7)

BUILDING PROCESSES THAT FOSTER VOLUNTEER RETENTION

Many years ago Jan Carlson, the head of Scandinavian Airlines, made an interesting observation about customer service. He noted that what was important in providing good service was not so much the absolute quality of the service as the perception that the customer had of the quality of the service. This subtle observation explains why sometimes you can be confident that you are doing a good job only to discover that those you are providing for have quite a different impression.

In many ways, a volunteer is another 'customer' of the charity. Much of what volunteers 'see and feel' as they relate to the organisation will be similar to their experiences with other types of customer relationships. McSweeney and Alexander (1996) commented:

> The first step in attracting new volunteers, and hopefully keeping them, requires us to look at ourselves, our organisation and structure from the perspective of the new entrant. What impressions do we create by the environment in which we work? What sort of general images do we portray as an organisation? How do we measure up in terms of friendliness and welcoming newcomers?

Volunteering and consumer behaviour

Charities that take volunteers for granted tend to overlook the fact that the volunteer is, in a sense, always judging their performance. When the performance reaches unacceptable levels, the volunteer, like any educated consumer, will go elsewhere. Keaveney et al (1991) described this as follows:

> Like any other customer, volunteers 'shop' for high quality volunteer experiences. Contrary to beliefs commonly held by dedicated managers and paid staff, the benefits of volunteering are not supplied by only one 'vendor' (i.e., nonprofit organization).

The extent of this 'shopping behaviour' is indicated in the results of a 2004 analysis of the VolunteerMatch online matching system (Peter D Hart Associates, 2004) which, in response to the question 'How many volunteer opportunities do you generally respond to before finding the right place to volunteer?', found the following patterns:

	%
● One	21
● Two or three	48
● Four to six	21
● Seven +	10

This might become institutionalised. The 2005 report by the Russell Commission in the UK contained a suggestion that one way to increase the credibility of volunteer opportunities among young people is to create a system of 'mystery shoppers' who would 'provide "undercover" assessments of volunteering opportunities' and share their results with their peers.

Most volunteer-involving organisations, alas, treat prospective volunteers as more of a mystery than a potential shopper. Ellis (2002) noted: 'It's amazing how many organizations totally undercut their recruitment efforts by ignoring what happens to prospects when they make the attempt to express interest in becoming a volunteer.'

One way to avoid this problem is to conduct a periodic audit of your services from the perspective of the customer, 'walking' through your system and looking at what you do and how you do it from the customer's point of view. This is most easily done by examining what are called 'Moments of Truth', interactions with the customer that allow them to form an opinion, either good or bad, about the quality of the service being provided.

Looking at volunteering from the customer's perspective

Some of these critical impressions can be formed before you are even aware of the customer's existence; others are formed during interactions with you or members of your agency's staff.

As a first example of this, Hobson and Malec (1999) conducted a test of the volunteer management processes of 500 charities affiliated with the United Way (an international network of non-profit organisations) in a mid-western city of the United States. The test involved phoning each charity in the guise of a prospective volunteer, with the intent of testing how the person who answered the phone call dealt with the would-be volunteer.

Here are some of their findings:

- Only 49.3% of callers received an offer of assistance ('May I help you?').
- 69.3% did not receive the name of the staff person answering the phone.
- 26.4% were not referred to the appropriate contact person.
- When the contact person was not available, only 48.7% of callers were asked for their name and phone number.
- Only 30% of callers received a return call after leaving their contact information.
- In 16.1% of calls, prospective volunteers were not thanked for contacting the agency.

Imagine the attitude created among prospective volunteers who receive this sort of treatment. They are most likely to form an opinion that the charity, even if it is advertising for volunteer assistance, is neither sincere nor competent. The inattentiveness and casual treatment clearly indicates to them that the charity would not be likely to value them if they were in fact to begin volunteering. That the charity's personnel are overworked, under-staffed and thoroughly frazzled is simply irrelevant to the perception that is formed – the prospective volunteer does not 'see' this.

And now imagine what kind of response you might receive if you called your own organisation posing as a potential volunteer ...

As a second example, consider the experience of Big Brothers Big Sisters (BBBS) in the United States when it conducted an assessment (Furano et al, 1993) of its internal processing system for volunteer applicants.

Since it matches adults with children in volunteering situations that are generally unsupervised, BBBS has long led the field in intensive background screening of volunteer applicants. These processes include criminal background checks, multiple interviews, psychological screening, home visits and other risk management procedures.

The internal assessment, however, revealed an unfortunate consequence of these procedures – they were incredibly lengthy. An applicant might apply and then spend as long as six months waiting for the screening processes to be completed. This came as a complete surprise to prospective volunteers, whose natural expectation was that they would begin volunteering relatively quickly, something they were initially eager to do.

From the standpoint of BBBS these screening techniques were necessary in order to ensure safe matches. It was, in fact, good management practice. From the standpoint of potential volunteers it was another story. Their reaction was one of feeling abandoned by the organisation after their initial good faith effort to help out. The result was a large hole in the retention system, occurring even before BBBS had officially accepted the volunteers.

A critical factor in this process was that prospective volunteers were not told in advance how long the processing might take and that for extended periods they might not learn anything from BBBS about how the background investigation was proceeding. They were essentially being left 'in the dark'.

Following a similar study of Big Brothers and Sisters in Canada, Northstar Research Partners (1999) recommended:

> These are barriers that occur after the individual has made the decision to volunteer, and something happens externally to prevent them from doing so. Some examples cited are:
> - Feeling 'put on the spot'.
> - On first contact, too much information was required from the volunteer, none was given to the volunteer.
> - Agency seemed to be looking for an 'ideal'.
> - Feelings of inadequacy in terms of skill.

Volunteers making first contact require reassurance and information. This study revealed that some felt alienated and inadequate after speaking to the agency for the first time.

Both recruitment and retention could potentially be improved by addressing some of the individual barriers and institutional barriers.

A similar result was found by Phillips et al (2002) in a study of motivations of Canadian volunteers:

> There was a clear sense that rules and screening procedures have become more onerous in recent years. Although all indicated that they understood the reasons for, and value of, police checks and other screening procedures for volunteers with access to children, sometimes the tone (the sense of being guilty until proven innocent) and length of time (months to receive word on a police check) made these processes annoying.

Similar difficulties exist in other areas of management when volunteers are delayed in being matched with clients or with work. Fahey et al (2003) noted the difficulty among volunteer ambulance officers in Tasmania in areas where the small number of new volunteers delayed training of new recruits for months. One volunteer who was interviewed commented: 'It takes typically eight to twelve months for a new recruit to become trained. Most of our volunteers are now "observers".'

Finn Paradis and Usui (1987) discovered that turnover increased among hospice volunteers because their interest in volunteering waned if they were not immediately placed into work assignments following training. The Institute for Volunteering Research in the UK found a similar result in 2003:

> Several respondents told us they had been discouraged from volunteering because organisations took so long to respond to an initial enquiry, process an application or place the respondent once they had been recruited. Without a prompt response, many potential volunteers may walk away: they may join another organisation, or worse, they may assume that they are not wanted as volunteers and never even try again.

Problems arising from the volunteer involvement process are not limited to new volunteers. Griffiths (2003) pointed to some interesting difficulties beginning to arise among meals on wheels volunteers in New South Wales. Recent changes in meals on wheels procedures have resulted in less time being available for each volunteer to deliver meals to those on their route. The results that Griffiths noted were:

> ... many of the volunteers commented that recent changes to Meals on Wheels operations and increased workload has affected the quality of the relationships that volunteers develop with recipients. One change that many volunteers commented on was that volunteers were not able to spend more than a few minutes with each recipient.

Besides reducing interpersonal contacts with clients, the change in procedures was also hampering the development of relationships among volunteers who delivered meals together, forcing them to rush through the entire route.

Situations such as these led Hobson et al to conclude in 2002 that: 'Most organizations are not "volunteer-friendly" and have tremendous room for improvement.'

Analysing volunteer management processes

The points of contact at which the customer tends to form judgements about the quality of a service are often referred to as 'Moments of Truth'. What follows is an attempt to guide you through a self-reflective examination of your volunteer management system, viewing it through the eyes and experiences of the volunteer. We will divide the examination into four stages:

1 The prospective volunteer's initial approach to the charity
2 The process of first interviewing and matching the volunteer with a position

3 The ongoing working relationship of a volunteer with the charity

4 The follow-up by the charity with volunteers who have completed their term of service

As you work through the questions consider:

- What perception is likely to be formed by a volunteer during this interaction?
- What can be done to shift that perception in a more positive direction?

1. Initial approach

This stage covers the first experiences of the prospective volunteer with the charity, sometimes before the charity is even aware of their interest.

Initial awareness

- Does the potential volunteer have an impression of your organisation and its operation before contact is made?
- Is this impression favourable, accurate and complete?
- What do others say about your organisation?
- How does the potential volunteer learn enough about you even to know that you are a possible source of voluntary work?
- Is your descriptive material readily accessible?
- Are your organisational materials available in languages matching the make-up of your community?
- Are those pictured in your materials representative of the community in which your organisation operates?
- Do materials outline what the volunteer can expect to receive and do they answer the initial questions that the volunteer is likely to have?
- Do materials give the potential volunteer a reason to choose your organisation rather than another one?
- Are your descriptive materials so crowded with detail that no one would be inclined to read them at all?
- How does the image of volunteering with you look to different cultures, age groups and populations from the ones you currently involve?

Approach to the organisation

- Is it easy for the potential volunteer to come to you?
- Are there multiple ways that a volunteer can contact you – phone, personal visit, website and so on?
- Are you located so that the volunteer can reach you easily?
- Do you look approachable?
- Are there clear directions to guide volunteers to those who will begin to interact with them?

- Have you considered setting up off-site contact points that might be more accessible to potential volunteers – at shopping areas, libraries, schools or other places where people congregate?

First contact

- Do all staff receive training on how to deal with a prospective volunteer?
- How are volunteers treated by the first person with whom they have contact?
- Does that person make them feel welcome?
- Can that person help them clarify their interest in volunteering?
- Does that person make them begin to understand the process through which they will become involved?
- Does that person verbally express interest and gratitude?
- Is there a set packet of introductory materials that can be sent to prospective volunteers to educate them about the charity?
- How long does it take to return phone calls from interested community members who have expressed an interest in volunteering?

2. Interviewing and matching

This stage covers the discussion between the charity and the volunteer about volunteering – the application process, volunteer interview and the decision about an appropriate volunteer position.

Internal referral

- Are potential volunteers efficiently referred to others for assistance, without giving them the impression that they are being shunted off on to someone else?
- Are they guided, rather than abandoned?
- If multiple referrals are necessary to resolve volunteers' questions, is there a clear reason for this which is explained to them?
- If the volunteers are referred to others, are they offered the choice of the member of staff phoning them rather than their having to phone back to the charity?
- If the primary volunteer programme contact is not available, how long is the delay before the prospective volunteer is phoned back?

Initial application

- How are potential volunteers initially treated by the person who will be responsible for working with them?
- Are prospective volunteers made to feel important and welcomed or do they feel as if they are imposing?
- Is care taken to understand the volunteer's needs and perspectives?

- Do volunteers feel as if they are the ones whose needs are paramount and that the intent of the organisation is to bend all resources to make them feel satisfied?
- Are attempts made to minimise paperwork which must be completed by the volunteer and to explain the purpose and need for all paperwork that remains?
- Is a prospective volunteer sent information about the organisation and its work to consider before coming in to discuss volunteering further?
- Are forms available in alternative formats for those with reading impairments – such as Braille or enlargeable computer files? Are forms available in alternative languages?

Negotiation and interviewing

- Is the initial volunteer interview conducted at a time and place convenient for the prospective volunteer?
- Is the location for the interview likely to put the prospective volunteer at ease?
- Is the interview conducted more as a friendly chat or an interrogation?
- During the negotiation process over the work to be performed, does the volunteer understand why the negotiation over time, screening requirements and so on, is taking place, and does the volunteer feel satisfied about the bargaining process and its outcomes?
- Are volunteers given options about their type of work and scheduling?
- Do volunteers feel that you are as interested in making this work for them as for you?
- If screening or placement procedures are lengthy, does the volunteer receive periodic contact updates?
- Is the prospective volunteer involved in ways other than directly volunteering during this waiting period – shadowing, observing and so on?

3. Ongoing working relationship

This stage concerns the ongoing interaction of the volunteer with the charity.

Working process

- Do volunteers understand the process through which their work will contribute and their role in that process?
- Are the roles and responsibilities of others with whom the volunteer will be working clearly spelt out?
- Are volunteers allowed to voice their opinions about how the work should be performed?
- Are these opinions regularly requested?

- Do volunteers feel that they are partners in what is going on?
- Do you attempt to keep paperwork that must be completed by the volunteer at a minimum?
- Do procedures assist volunteers in developing relationships with other volunteers, clients and staff or deter them from doing so?

Updating

- Are efforts made to keep the volunteer informed about the progress of the charity?
- Are these efforts carried out by the organisation or does the volunteer have to initiate them?
- Are volunteers informed of developments which will impact on their ability to work?
- Is the volunteer invited to meetings in which the conduct of the charity is discussed and at which decisions are made?
- Does the volunteer participate in making these decisions?
- If key aspects of the work assignment change, is the volunteer informed of the need for these changes?
- Do volunteers participate in determining how their own roles might change or develop over time?

Delivery of product

- Are volunteers given feedback about the performance of their work on a regular basis?
- Is this feedback designed to allow the volunteer to perform the work more effectively?
- Does the volunteer receive supervisory time and attention?
- Are volunteers recognised for their contribution on both a formal and informal basis?
- Is this recognition given in a way that shows respect for the volunteer?
- Are volunteers asked to provide their own feedback about the quality of the work being performed?
- Are volunteers empowered to add their own thoughts and input into the way work is done and the type of work they are assigned?

4. Follow-up

This final stage concerns the relationship between the volunteer and the charity after the volunteer has completed their initial term of service, including after the volunteer has moved on.

Departure

- Do volunteers perceive that the organisation has enjoyed their participation and would like them to continue the relationship?
- Are volunteers made to feel as though they may return to the organisation, even if they are interested in changing their volunteer assignment?
- Are these options explained to volunteers far enough in advance for them to consider their interests?
- Is an exit interview conducted to determine why a volunteer wants to leave?

Follow-up

- Are real attempts made to contact volunteers who have completed their commitment in order to update them about services that have been given?
- Is additional information which might be helpful routinely sent to potential repeat volunteers?
- Are they kept on newsletter lists?
- Are they invited to activities or volunteer recognition events?

Continuing contacts

- How are volunteers greeted and treated if they approach the organisation for a second time?
- Are they remembered, recognised and greeted as old friends or do they start all over again?
- Are records kept of volunteer service that will identify who has volunteered before and indicate what they were involved in?
- Are records kept of those who previously received services or participated in the programme as clients who might come back in later years to 'give back' as volunteers?

When examining these points, do not be limited to the questions above. Your examination should essentially 'track' volunteers through all the processes they encounter as they work with your organisation. Put yourself in the volunteers' place, view what is happening from their perspective and analyse how confusing or cumbersome the process may appear to them.

One of the best ways to undertake this analysis is to involve new volunteers, many of whom will have distinct memories of what they found unfamiliar or uncomfortable. While some of these items seem insignificant, each of them can create a barrier that leads to the loss of volunteers.

Undertaking this analysis can tell you a lot about why you may be 'losing' volunteers, especially if you seem to have poor retention during the early stages of volunteer involvement.

The team approach to analysing volunteer systems

The tricky aspect of looking at internal process is that it is difficult for those who created the process to realise how it really looks to others. Those on the inside are more likely to understand the intricacies of a process and more likely to believe it works, mostly because they produced it. In addition, organisational processes tend to go through an interesting mutation over time. Processes are originally developed for efficiency and providing a service. As time goes on, however, these processes tend to be 'improved' by those who are administering them – and generally improved to meet internal needs (that is, what works 'best' for staff) rather than external ones (what would work best for clients and others).

Accordingly, it is wise to involve a team of people when analysing processes. The team should optimally include:

- the volunteer programme manager
- an experienced volunteer
- a new volunteer
- agency staff who work with volunteers.

Ilsley (1990) commented on the use of volunteers in this effort:

> Procedures that can benefit from volunteer input include volunteer selection, orientation, pre- and in-service training programs, task assignment, and meetings. Because volunteers are directly involved in all these procedures, they are uniquely qualified to know which ways of carrying out the procedures work and which do not.

It is also very valuable to have input from total outsiders, especially if the organisation is attempting to recruit from new population groups. Representatives of these groups may very well notice aspects of your procedures that are invisible to those already involved with the programme.

Answering volunteers' unasked questions

Often, prospective volunteers have questions about the operation of a programme or about possible requirements but are unwilling to ask these questions directly. They may involve issues around: 'Will I have to do that?' 'What are my options?' or similar concerns. Especially among population groups not experienced in volunteering, they may lack any information on how even to begin attempting to volunteer. Lasby (2004) noted the percentage of the population in different age categories who cited as a barrier to volunteering that they 'Do not know how':

Age	%
15–24	29
25–34	22
35–44	18
45–54	17
55–64	16
65+	15

One way to avoid this dilemma is to anticipate questions and provide the answers without waiting for them to be asked.

As an example of this technique, here are some of the issues addressed on the website of the Indy Hospice Volunteers Programme (www.transporting.to/IndyHospiceVolunteers/volunteer.html).

Requirements of potential volunteers
- Completion of application
- Two written references on file
- Criminal background check
- Completion of volunteer training
- TB test or chest x-ray with negative results **
- Completion of OSHA (Occupational Safety and Health Administration) requirements **
- Hepatitis B vaccine or a written statement declining the vaccine **
- Signed Confidentiality Statement form

** Indicates patient care volunteers only.

A person who volunteers is trained for the area in which they choose to serve. There are three areas with different classifications within those areas.

I   Administration Volunteer is a person who wants to volunteer but wants no direct patient contact. They may provide administrative assistance in the office setting. They may work at home doing paperwork . There are also volunteers who sew, knit and crochet projects during the year for patients. There are non-patient care volunteers who mow garden lawns, shovel snow, run errands and so on. They require a three-hour orientation training class.

II Patient Care Volunteer is a person who wants to volunteer directly with patients, whether it is in the patient's own home, primary care giver's home, assisted living home or nursing home. They require twelve hours of orientation training.

III Bereavement Volunteer is a person who wants to volunteer to go through the bereavement process with the patient and the family. This volunteer may start at the onset of accepting hospice services and continue with the family thirteen months after the passing of their loved one. They require eighteen hours of orientation training.

For an extremely useful and fun version of this approach, see the Volunteer FAQ for Burning Man at www.burningman.com/participate/volunteer_faq.html. In addition to providing basic logistical information it includes motivating advice to potential volunteers:

When volunteering during the event, please be careful to not double-book yourself or spread yourself too thin. Remember to schedule some relaxation and play time into your day. First-time burners tend to suffer from a condition know as the 'Ack! factor' and find themselves over-stimulated. Be careful not to over-extend yourself. If you volunteer and really enjoy it, you can always offer to come back and fill in for more shifts.

It is easy to see how providing the volunteer with the above information helps to reduce any doubts or concerns that the prospective volunteer might have. Providing this information in advance both serves to educate volunteers about their options and avoids unnecessary fears deterring them from making a commitment.

Unasked questions can also be addressed during the interviewing process, as noted by the Federal Emergency Management Agency (FEMA) (1995):

Potential recruits may have a number of concerns about themselves and the EMS [Emergency Medical Service] organization that they do not express. The interviewer must ensure that these 'unasked questions' are addressed:

- What do I really have to do? Can I manage it? Do I have the skill? Can I handle it emotionally?
- How much time will it demand? Is there enough to keep me interested? Will it put pressure on my regular job or family?
- What danger will I be in? What are the risks?
- Who benefits? Why should I do this?

Explaining internal processes to volunteers

Another key area to developing user-friendly processes is ensuring that volunteers receive a good explanation of what is being done and why it is being done, particularly as this relates to them. Interviews of prospective volunteers are a good time to provide some of this explanation and, in particular, to explain to volunteers what steps will need to be taken from the time of the interview until their official placement as volunteers, and an approximate timeframe for these steps.

As screening processes for potential volunteers have become more common, more onerous and more time-consuming we have created a necessary but unfortunate bottleneck between the desire of the motivated prospective volunteer to begin work and our risk management procedures. This bottleneck can lead to unfortunate results if volunteers are not aware of it and begin to suspect that they have been abandoned by the charity.

Here is an example of such an explanation, in this case utilised by the Girl Guides of Canada, where a complete screening process may take up to six months:

> Tell the potential applicant:
> - The steps in our screening process.
> - That acceptance is not automatic and that decisions are based on our assessment of an applicant's ability to meet the requirements of the position, based on a written position description. These requirements may include specific skills and competencies, and may also include traits of character and temperament.
> - That further screening may be necessary depending on position requirements. Applicants may be required to submit proof of qualifications, technical ability, experience, license or certification as a condition of acceptance, and from time to time thereafter as appropriate to the requirements of the position. These may include driver license checks, driver abstracts, vehicle insurance, credit checks for those (other than Unit Guiders) handling money, or other checks relevant to the position.
> - That screening is ongoing and continues for as long as an individual is in Guiding.

This provides the prospective volunteer with a sense of context of what will happen in screening, why it will happen and what to expect in the future. It also serves to shape the expectations of prospective volunteers and gives them a sense of understanding that will help them maintain a positive outlook.

The critical first contact with prospective volunteers

Often the opinions of a volunteer are shaped in the very first instance of contact with an organisation. Cihlar (2004) commented: 'The volunteer's initial interaction with programme staff sets the tone for the entire volunteer experience.' This is especially true if prospective volunteers are unfamiliar with volunteering or have reason to doubt in any way the reception that they will receive. It can be particularly true of groups whose experiences with large organisations have not always been positive.

As Gaskin (2003) noted:

> Volunteers are nervous at their first enquiry or interview. They want a satisfying personal interaction in which the person representing the organisation takes the time to find out what their interests, capabilities and inclinations are, to explain what is available and what is expected and to suggest suitable opportunities.

Gaskin went on to make some useful suggestions about making this first contact a good one:

- well-staffed reception and walk-in/call-in/email access
- a friendly and efficient initial response
- attractive handouts in multiple languages, as appropriate, to be taken away
- informal but efficient process with attentive personalised treatment
- volunteer role descriptions
- a volunteer charter and/or clear explanations of rights and responsibilities, procedures and expectations
- individualised matching to opportunities
- as wide a range of volunteers' roles as possible
- referral elsewhere if an appropriate opportunity cannot be found.

Remember the wise old saying: 'You never get a second chance to make a good first impression.'

Examples of this initial first impression contact might include:

- initial call to an agency about volunteering
- first meeting or interview with volunteer manager
- orientation session
- first day on volunteer assignment.

During each of these moments, volunteers are forming opinions about whether the somewhat risky move they are considering (offering themselves to a strange organisation) is a wise choice. At this point, any feeling of discomfort is likely to be magnified in the mind of the volunteer and any sense that the agency is indifferent or uninterested is highly likely to result in the volunteer ending the relationship as quickly as possible. At this early and quite fragile point in the relationship, the potential volunteer is highly attuned to any signs of welcome or rejection. A potential volunteer who is not made to feel welcome by a harried receptionist may form an impression of the organisation from which it never recovers. New volunteers who are ignored by busy staff on their first day at work often conclude that they are not really wanted.

It is difficult to estimate how many organisations suffer from not looking approachable to potential volunteers. Some suggestion of the magnitude of this problem can be estimated through examining the popularity of the new Internet sites for matching prospective volunteers to volunteer opportunities. These sites tend to be very user friendly and very safe from the perspective of potential volunteers – they can look before they leap. A report by GoVolunteer (2004), the Australian matching system, reveals that 44% of those using the site had never volunteered before. Many of these are under age 25 and a significant percentage of them are foreign born – groups who may reasonably worry about directly contacting an agency in person.

A report on VolunteerMatch, the major US Internet matching site, noted that 75% of users had not volunteered before (Peter D Hart Research Associates, 2004). While some of this might be explained by the ease or novelty of using the Internet, it is likely that many prospective volunteers found this method less frightening than approaching an agency directly and facing the possibility of rejection. They certainly found it more convenient.

It is also critical to realise that 'first contact' may occur in a variety of ways and at a variety of times, some of these applying to volunteers who have been in the organisation for some time. When volunteers assume new duties or work with new units within the organisation they are in a 'first contact' situation and may feel uncomfortable. Sadler and Marty (1998) found this among hospice volunteers who occasionally felt reluctant to interact equally with hospice staff whom they felt had more expertise than they. Sadler and Marty noted the implications for a setting intended to honour the volunteer but which can result in the volunteer feeling out of place if care is not taken:

> For some volunteers, feelings of uncomfortableness in discussing their patients with the experienced hospice staff led to partial feelings of isolation from the organization. For others, a positive team experience enhanced their identification to the hospice. The potential message to hospice staff is quite clear: it is important to make sure that volunteers attending team meetings are made to feel as much of an 'expert' as the others at the meeting. Hospice staff cannot instantly assume that a volunteer at a team meeting is simply another member of the staff at the meeting.

Involving new volunteer populations

Some categories of volunteers, such as young people or minorities who are already uncertain about their reception by the organisation, are extremely sensitive to telltale behaviour patterns that might 'reveal' the true intent of the organisation. These other populations include not only young people and ethnic or cultural minorities, but also those with disabilities, emigrant populations or others outside the social and economic mainstream.

Heyworth and Fryar (2004) noted:

> Too frequently it is possible to find volunteer programs and even managers of volunteer programs who quite willingly say they are accepting of volunteers from CALD [culturally and linguistically diverse] backgrounds, however the reality is that their practices state the opposite. Organisational culture, the attitudes of other volunteers and paid staff and the tasks a CALD volunteer is asked to undertake, may in fact all transmit quite a different message.

Raskoff and Sundeen (1999), in a study of youth community service programmes in Los Angeles, found that:

> Among the responses that indicate some fear, the students most frequently admitted the fear of making mistakes and the fear of being rejected in their service activities. Nonsectarian school students showed the greatest concern about the former and religious school students about the latter. Neither of these concerns appears unusual for adolescents who may find themselves in new or different environments.

Over half of respondents indicated some degree of fear.

In a 2003 survey the Institute for Volunteering Research in the UK uncovered the following potential barriers to volunteer involvement perceived by populations not commonly involved in volunteering:

- Lack of confidence was found to be a key barrier. It was exacerbated for individuals who had experienced exclusion in other areas of life, and when volunteering took place in unfamiliar environments.
- Delays in the recruitment process were particularly discouraging – without a prompt response it was apparent that some potential volunteers would simply walk away.
- A physically inaccessible environment created an obvious barrier, particularly for disabled people with mobility-related impairments.

They also noted that solving these potential barriers is not impossible:

> By ensuring that recruitment-processes were user-friendly – minimising form filling and asking new recruits in for a chat rather than an interview, for example – some organisations had successfully made the volunteering experience seem less daunting.

Pankaj (2002) in a survey of ethnic volunteering in Scotland found:

> Only 13% of responding VCs [volunteer centres] and 35% of VIOs [volunteer involving organisations] provide information in more than one language. Some organisations only provide such information on request. One VC (within Glasgow) has established a pool of volunteer interpreters to provide initial support to registering volunteers if needed.

Clark (2003), in a very useful work on involving volunteers with mental illness, suggested the following customer-friendly actions that would work equally well with other populations:

- Include the volunteer's support staff (e.g. key workers) in the process.
- Work in partnership with community bridge builders and supported volunteering practitioners.
- Run open 'taster' sessions prior to volunteering.
- Identify a named member of staff with specialist knowledge of mental health issues.
- Encourage trial volunteering periods.
- Develop graduated activities that increase responsibility over time.
- Run pre-volunteering training courses.
- Develop peer group support and regular group supervision sessions.
- Involve all volunteers in peer mentoring and buddying systems.

The above are all examples of 'transitional strategies' which make it more likely that a prospective volunteer will feel comfortable establishing a more formal relationship with an organisation.

Hobbs (2000), discussing the involvement of Latino volunteers, noted that the appearance of the organisation and its offices can make a difference:

> The organization's meeting and work spaces should reflect a diversity of cultures, in particular the Latino culture. This can be accomplished by such simple things as the choice of prints you hang on the wall, the artwork on your calendar, the decorative objects on tables and shelves.

While paperwork is often a barrier for populations from different languages and cultures, do not assume they are the only ones for whom it poses a problem. Aitken (2000) referred to a study of emergency services volunteers in western Australia that suggested up to 20% of them had some form of literacy problems, with five to seven per cent having severe problems.

Tips for a volunteer-friendly organisation

Here are six specific suggestions for maximising the likelihood of a volunteer gaining a positive first impression:

1   Make sure that those answering the phone in your organisation know about the volunteer programme and project an organised and friendly attitude to callers asking about volunteering. Test this by occasionally phoning in and seeing how well this is working. It is impossible to overstate how important this first call can be or how devastating the impact if it is handled poorly.

2   Make sure you phone back those who ring in about volunteer opportunities as quickly as possible. There is a substantial decay factor in volunteer enthusiasm over small amounts of time and this decay can quickly lead to a firm conclusion that the charity is not really interested. If you are too busy to process the volunteer's request immediately, then at least phone them back to acknowledge their interest and arrange a later time for a longer conversation about the recruitment process.

3   If your agency is difficult to locate or has limited parking, considering setting up a volunteer kiosk at a convenient location – a shopping centre, library or other gathering point. This will make it easy for potential volunteers to begin the process of connecting with you.

4   When first meeting people, strive to give them a sense of understanding of the process they will be going through in applying to become a volunteer. This is especially important in these times when background checks can consume weeks. A volunteer who feels 'lost' during this initial phase will quickly become lost.

5   Strive to give the new volunteer a sense of inclusion, establishing immediate social connections with staff and other volunteers. One simple way to do this is to walk them through the office and introduce them to others, particularly those with whom they will be working.

6   Make the volunteer's first day at the organisation a ceremonial one, with an official greeting and thanks. This will tend to put the official seal of approval on the volunteer's decision.

While many of these changes may seem minor, their cumulative effect will be significant.

Do not, however, assume that you need only take care with prospective or new volunteers. Even dedicated customers have been known to change their shopping habits. Conducting a rigorous and complete analysis of what happens with experienced volunteers prevents you from taking their commitment for granted and pushes you to find ways to keep streamlining your system so that it continues to meet their needs.

chapter 8

SUSTAINING RETENTION ALONG THE VOLUNTEER LIFE CYCLE

Thinking longitudinally about volunteer involvement

Most studies of volunteer motivation have concentrated on examining the factors that influence the decision to initiate volunteering. These factors are complex, as Miller (1985) noted: 'A volunteer's involvement and satisfaction derive from a complex combination of the volunteer's personality, the nature of the volunteer activity, and the nature of the volunteer's other activities.'

These studies, however, are not particularly useful in then determining what factors might influence that same volunteer's decision to continue volunteering within an organisation. This deficiency arises because initial motivations can be quite different from subsequent attitudes and behaviour, which are based on a wide variety of factors. Ilsley (1990), in his invaluable series of interviews with volunteers, found that:

> Inexperienced volunteers, defined as those who have been in service for less than six months, usually can explain their reasons for volunteering without hesitation and can describe tangible ways in which they expect to be rewarded for their work ... Experienced volunteers, by contrast, sometimes have difficulty explaining why they continue their work. A volunteer who had worked at a museum for fifteen years said, 'I've been here so long I can't remember why I stay.'

This situation is further complicated by the fact that volunteers' motivations, reactions to their volunteer tasks and adjustment to other life factors tend to change over time (Omoto et al, 2000). Selbee and Reed (2001) commented: 'a complex interplay of factors encourages or inhibits volunteering depending on the combination of an individual's life cycle circumstances.'

Changes in life cycle can trigger a re-examination by volunteers of their commitment. As the situations of volunteers change, their reactions to volunteering and their motivational needs also change.

Over the length of a volunteer's relationship with an organisation, there will tend to occur numerous critical incident points at which the volunteer will review their decision to continue volunteering. These points seem to have some predictability, both in time of occurrence and in the content of the factors that influence the volunteer in either leaving or staying, but are often ignored in studies of volunteer motivation. Dailey, writing in 1986, noted that 'researchers need to recognize there is a wide range of behaviors and attitudes that materialize and drive volunteer activity well after the decision to join and donate energy and time have been made.'

This chapter reviews these critical points and suggests ways for a volunteer programme manager to influence the volunteer's decision during this process of self-examination. Please note that the timeframes given in this chapter are highly variable, both in terms of differences among individual volunteers and in terms of variations based on when things are done within an organisation. Some organisations, for example, have long entry periods for volunteers, in which months may pass between initial acceptance and actually beginning work. The timeframes utilised in this chapter begin to run from the time when the volunteers first engage in actually doing some type of volunteer assignment. They will then vary based on the frequency with which that volunteer is engaged in the work – greater frequency tends to shorten the time periods; infrequent connection with work tends to extend some of the earlier timeframes. After you have a feel for the different timeframes below you should find it easy to estimate their period of occurrence within your organisation.

The volunteer's first month

During their first month in a new position, volunteers are learning about the assignment that they have been given. A volunteer manager should always view this initial matching as a hopeful but occasionally incorrect experiment, commonly based on a relatively short interview in which each participant is operating with a great deal of ignorance about the other. The primary factor influencing volunteers during this critical time is one of 'job comfort', that is, do they feel capable and interested in the work now that they are actually learning what it is really about? Reality has replaced the job description. Volunteers who discover that the position to which they have been assigned is not one in which they feel comfortable will start to disappear.

A clever volunteer manager can easily control any danger during this period by deliberately scheduling a 'review interview' about 30 days after the initial placement. This interview, arranged at the time of initial placement, is explained as an opportunity for volunteers to decide whether they really like the work. The first month basically operates as a 'test drive' for volunteers to be exposed to the actual work and to determine whether they are comfortable with their ability and interest in continuing in that position.

While this creates some additional work for volunteer managers, it enables them to 'fine-tune' placement decisions, based both on the volunteer's new knowledge about the work and the agency's new knowledge about the volunteer.

As every experienced volunteer manager knows, making a 'perfect match' in placement is essential for smooth working relationships.

The volunteer's first six months

Following the initial 'nose to the grindstone' period in which volunteers concentrate on learning about their positions, they will tend to raise their heads and look around at the broader elements in their relationship with the organisation, and to begin to form judgements about how things are going. As an example, however, of how circumstances can slightly alter the timeframe we are discussing, if the volunteer assignment includes moving the volunteer to a new location, then what is discussed in this section may well occur earlier in the volunteer experience.

Critical factors include:

■ **Reality versus expectation**
  Does the situation in which volunteers are now engaged meet their expectations in a positive way? Are they gaining what they thought they would from volunteering? Is the volunteers' work vastly different from what they thought or what they were told during initial induction and training? Do the clients and work environment meet the expectations of the volunteer?

■ **Assignment fit**
  Do the overall aspects of the assignment (client relations, work process and so on) match with the volunteer's interests and abilities? Does the volunteer feel equal to the work and capable of achieving some success at it?

■ **Life fit**
  Do the volunteering role and its time and logistical requirements fit comfortably into the rest of the volunteer's life, work and relationships? Is the volunteering role too demanding or too intrusive?

■ **Social fit**

Do volunteers feel as though they are becoming an accepted part of the organisation's social environment? Do they feel respected and a part of the team? Are they making friends and meeting colleagues?

Possible solutions for helping a volunteer to reach a positive conclusion during this period include:

1   During interviewing of volunteers explore their perceptions of what the experience will be like. If these expectations are unrealistic, educate the volunteers as to what the experience will actually be. This is particularly important if there are unrealistic expectations of relationships with the client or the degree of success that can be expected in a short time.

2   Create a buddy or mentor system for new volunteers. These assigned colleagues will assume responsibility for answering any questions that volunteers have, helping them with their new roles, and introducing them to the social fabric of the organisation. Experienced volunteers make excellent buddies and mentors. Note, however, that being a buddy is different from being a supervisor. The role of the buddy is primarily to help the new person become comfortable, not to manage them.

3   Assume that you (or their supervisor) will need to allocate more time for communication with new volunteers and schedule this in accordingly. Do not assume that the volunteer will come to you; instead, create opportunities to talk to the volunteer, even if it is just a 'social call'.

4   Schedule a six-month review. This is not so much an evaluation as a chance to talk to the volunteer in a formal way about how they are feeling and whether they are enjoying themselves. If you have assigned the volunteer to work with a staff supervisor, this review is an excellent opportunity to see how that relationship is developing. During the review explore how volunteering is impacting on the rest of the volunteer's life and how others are reacting to the fact that the person is now volunteering.

5   Give the volunteer symbols of belonging to the organisation. This can include a business card, a voice or postal mailbox or e-mail address, clothing or equipment. These symbols will reinforce the notion that the volunteer is part of the organisation. If others in the organisation have given you positive feedback about the volunteer, convey that information to the volunteer.

First anniversary/end of initial term or commitment

This is one of the most serious critical incident points because the volunteer may have fulfilled their initial time commitment and must now make an affirmative decision to renew that commitment as opposed to seeking a new volunteer opportunity.

Key factors for the volunteer at this time are:

- **Bonding**

   Has the volunteer developed favourable personal relationships with others in the organisation? Does the volunteer have friends among the other staff and volunteers?

- **Accomplishment/expectation**

   In reviewing their tenure, do volunteers feel that they have accomplished what they thought they would accomplish during the assignment? Do they feel successful, or do they feel that they have 'failed' to achieve what they wanted, either in serving the community or helping a particular client?

- **Opportunity for growth**

   In contemplating continuation of a volunteering role, does the volunteer look forward with anticipation or do they feel that the given tasks will simply be more of the same? Do volunteers feel that they have the opportunity for continued challenge in the position or does it appear boring?

Here are six management actions to assist a volunteer at this stage:

1   Develop a 'volunteer growth plan' for each volunteer. This plan, developed with and by each volunteer, will chart out how volunteers are feeling about their work and what might be done to re-kindle their interest if it is flagging. You will find suggestions about developing the growth plan on page 118.

2   Celebrate volunteers' terms of service, finding a way to show them what they have accomplished and how they are appreciated. Have testimonials from those with whom they have been working and examples of their accomplishments. Do not make the party seem as if you are giving them the gold retirement watch; instead make the theme 'Many happy returns'.

3   Make sure volunteers have an opportunity to see the results of their work and of the overall work of the organisation, preferably in a face-to-face encounter that conveys the real impact. A 1990 study of crisis centre volunteers found a substantial difference in average volunteer tenure in centres where volunteers had opportunities for face-to-face interventions with clients compared with those where the volunteers had little client contact. Always remember that the ultimate impact on the client is part of a volunteer's motivation, and it is difficult to feel motivated when you never know the results. Organisations that engage in outcome-based evaluations should be sure to inform volunteers about the results of these evaluations.

4   Strengthen the bonds of the volunteers to the organisation by giving them token items that symbolise 'belonging', for example, you might give them a photo album of them working with others, or mementos of past work.

5   Talk frankly to volunteers about whether they are still enjoying their work. Many volunteers will be reluctant to tell you this, either out of fear of seeming to let the organisation down or fear of seeming to criticise those with whom they work. Strive for an understanding with each volunteer that this discussion is not about 'failure', but about 'renewal', an opportunity to be even more successful in the future. Stress to all volunteers that ensuring that they enjoy and benefit from the type of work they do is a key goal in your involvement of volunteers. Remind them continually that they can support you in a variety of ways.

6   Be prepared with a number of different options for volunteers that can serve to re-kindle the sense of excitement they once had. These might include a change to a new position, a 'promotion' in their current position or even a sabbatical to step aside from their volunteering role and gain a new perspective or just a feeling of re-invigoration. Volunteers can easily be 'promoted' by giving them additional responsibilities, such as assisting in training other volunteers or serving as mentors or resources.

The volunteer's longer-term involvement

One of the key facts about volunteers who continue volunteering with an organisation for long periods is that they are likely to experience elements of change in their own lives that can impact on their attitude towards their volunteer experience. These alterations in their style of life or work will produce changes in their preferred approach to volunteering – particularly in the style of volunteering and the type of volunteer activity that they may prefer.

Hanawi (1990) noted this in an investigation of older volunteers who had been involved in volunteering for most of their lives:

> If one were to look at some of the volunteers in this study, one would find they were seeking, and were satisfied with, quite different aspects of volunteering at different points in their lives. These differences had nothing to do with changes in their values, but rather with changes in the character of their employment or some other aspect of their lives.

In the longer term, all individual volunteers will face critical incident points, major shifts in life or work style that affect their overall needs and motivations. Some of these will relate directly to what the volunteer is doing within the organisational context; others may be more related to other aspects of the volunteer's life. They are not always predictable, occurring at different times for different volunteers.

Here are some of the factors that will create these incidents:

■ **Assignment adjustment**
If the volunteer's assignment changes in any substantial way, then the volunteer's relation to the assignment may also change. This could include a change in the client to whom the volunteer is assigned or a change in the staff with whom the volunteer is working. It can very often include a change in the status of some other volunteer with whom there is a close attachment. It can also include a change in the paid employment or status of volunteers, resulting in a reassessment of the type of volunteer 'work' they would prefer.

■ **Life fit**
As the volunteers age, their own life and needs change. Critical change points include birth of children, change in paid employment, marriage, death of spouse, retirement and so on.

As Pearce noted in 1993:

> Volunteers may quit because of personal changes, such as moving or returning to work or school. Since volunteering is often viewed as a peripheral activity, it may be influenced more heavily by outside events than employment is.

A volunteer manager should stay attuned to how the volunteer's own life is going, since major changes in it will create critical examination of the volunteer's involvement with the agency. One very common example of this is the tendency of leaders in 4-H (a North American youth club) to depart when their children are no longer of an age to participate in 4-H activities (White and Arnold, 2003).

Two strategies are crucial in ensuring that volunteers remain committed during these changes:

1 Giving volunteers a sense of empowerment in shaping their volunteering role – if volunteers know they can discuss their tasks and have the opportunity to redesign them to fit a changing situation, they are more likely to remain.

2 Making each volunteer a 'true believer' in the cause of the organisation – perhaps the greatest factor in volunteer retention is the extent to which the volunteer truly believes in the work being done by the organisation. Volunteers who initially join for other reasons (social factors, job experience and so on) should be deliberately engaged in conversations about the need for the agency and its work.

While all this may seem like additional work, these suggestions are designed to allow the volunteer manager to concentrate on an essential task – retaining good volunteers. It is expensive and time-consuming for an agency to continue to have to recruit new volunteers. To determine whether you need to pay more attention to volunteer retention, you might consider keeping retention statistics on your volunteers and, in particular, graphing the approximate timeframe of their points of departure. If you begin to see clusters of departures around the timeframes above, then improving your statistics can be a simple task.

This process requires you to look at your volunteers on a longitudinal basis, remembering that, like all of us, they are likely to grow and change over time. Since volunteering depends upon meeting both the needs and circumstances of the volunteer, it makes sense that volunteer management will need to adjust to changes in those needs and circumstances.

Developing a volunteer growth plan

One method for encouraging volunteers to help design a volunteer experience that will continue to motivate them is to encourage them to develop a 'growth plan' as part of their annual evaluation process. This growth plan encourages volunteers to review the experience of the past year of volunteering and think about how they might better design the volunteer role that will best motivate them during the forthcoming year.

This discussion, facilitated by the volunteer programme manager, can revolve around a series of questions:

Work satisfaction questions

- What were you hoping to accomplish in your volunteer role this year?
- What were your greatest accomplishments while volunteering this year?
- What was your greatest frustration while volunteering this year?
- What would you do differently if you were to do your voluntary work this year again?
- What strengths, skills or talents did you discover or strengthen this year?
- How challenging and interesting do you find your work at this time?

Personal satisfaction questions

- What do you find most rewarding about volunteering here?
- What new friendships did you make here this year?
- How well do you think we are accomplishing our mission?
- What is your vision for what we ought to be doing to be more successful in the next five years?

Future growth questions

- What do you want to accomplish in your work next year?
- What do you want to accomplish personally next year?

- How can we best help you accomplish these goals?
- What kind of volunteer role would most help you attain these goals?
- What training or experience can we offer you to make you better able to fulfil your role?
- How can we make your time here more fulfilling?

The utility of this approach is best illustrated by the findings of a 1998 study by the US youth-volunteer group, DoSomething, which determined that 84% of organisations that give volunteers input into what they actually spend their time doing kept their volunteers for two or more years on average, compared with only 50% of those that offer volunteers little or no input.

HANDLING VOLUNTEER BURNOUT

The incidence of burnout among volunteers

One of the reasons volunteers may leave a programme is that they feel 'burnt out' or suffer from a lesser syndrome sometimes referred to as 'compassion fatigue'. In such instances, the volunteer will be hard to re-recruit, since the volunteer experience will be associated with that unpleasant feeling. Burnout is more likely to be related to the work being done by the volunteer than who the volunteer is.

Claxton et al (1998) noted that burnout in a group of volunteer 'buddies' in an AIDS programme was not related to either the initial motivations of the volunteers or to any demographic factors. Guinan et al (1991) identified emotional overload, client problems, lack of support and lack of training as stress factors for AIDS volunteers. Yan and Tang (2003) identified lack of personal accomplishment and emotional depletion as factors in burnout.

However, Yuffe (1998) commented that the personality characteristics that many volunteers have make them inherently subject to burnout:

> Volunteers who work in the helping professions are not immune from grieving. By their very nature they choose this volunteer work because they care deeply and compassionately about others. Because of this commitment they may ignore their own emotional health, leading to problems of overload, diminished activity and burn-out.

Burnout among volunteers is most probable when:

- the volunteer assignment is ambiguous, especially as it relates to the precise role of the volunteer
- the assignment is psychologically stressful
- the assignment leads to depersonalisation of the client group, either through bad relationships with difficult clients or relationships that end with a bad result for the client
- the volunteer is feeling a lack of accomplishment or success and interprets this as failure

- the volunteer feels a lack of organisational support and may even view the organisation as hindering efforts to provide assistance
- volunteers feel that the situation is beyond their control, through size, volume or complexity.

Burnout can lead directly to problems in volunteer retention. Ross et al (1999) found that one of the best predictors of dropping out was stress, such as that caused by client problems, role ambiguity, emotional overload and organisational factors, coupled with intensified depersonalisation as a reaction to this stress.

Burnout is prevalent among AIDS and hospice volunteer programmes, but exists as well in almost all others. In a 2001 study, 24% of Court Appointed Special Advocate programmes mentioned 'burnout' as a cause of volunteer departure. Byron and Curtis (2002) found significant evidence of burnout among watershed volunteers (who work in the area of conservation and the environment) in Australia.

A study of volunteering in the United States in 2003 by the Bureau of Labor Statistics noted that 2.4% of volunteers listed 'burnout' as their reason for discontinuing volunteering during the past year – almost 90,000 volunteers in a single year. A 2002 survey by the National Volunteer and Philanthropy Centre of Singapore reported that 18% of respondents reported 'feeling tired/burnt out' as a reason for discontinuing volunteering.

Part of this may simply be attributable to increased workloads placed on volunteers. The 2000 National Survey of Giving, Volunteering and Participation (NSGVP) in Canada (Hall et al 2001) reported that: 'in 2000, the average annual number of hours contributed per volunteer increased to 162 hours from 149 hours in 1997.' What makes this more telling is the fact that many of the volunteer hours were given by a relatively small group of 'super-volunteers' who far exceeded the average figure of freely given hours. The NSGVP indicated: 'It should be noted, however, that the top quarter of volunteers in 2000 contributed more hours, on average, than did their counterparts in 1997 (471 in 2000 compared with 431 in 1997).'

Fahey and Walker (2001) noted that among volunteer ambulance officers (VAOs) in Tasmania: 'VAO spend an average of 72 hours on-call per month, which equals the average number of hours worked by Australian volunteers per annum.' Increased demands on time are particularly increasing for leadership volunteers. In a report on fire brigade volunteers in New Zealand (UMR Research, 2001) noted:

A significant number of volunteers feel they spend too much time on their volunteer responsibilities. Significantly, chiefs and officers are most likely to feel overburdened by fire service responsibilities.

Many volunteer positions are inherently stressful, mandating that volunteer organisations establish systems for assisting their volunteers to cope, as was noted in regard to emergency medical services (EMS) volunteers in the United States (FEMA, 1995):

> There are so many incidents that an EMS person responds to that could affect the psyche of the volunteer that it is necessary for the EMS organization to have a system in place to care for the emotional well-being of its volunteers. Volunteers who respond to these life-threatening emergencies are subject not only to the stresses of life but also to the effects of being exposed to excessive risks, destruction, and human misery. The effect of this stress can be seen in the premature resignation of the volunteer or disruption of their health and happiness.

Smith (2004), in a study of rescue and recovery workers and volunteers at the World Trade Center clean-up, found that 20% reported symptoms that met the standards for Post-Traumatic Stress Disorder (PTSD), approximately four times the reported lifetime prevalence of PTSD in the general male population.

Burnout is particularly likely when only a small portion of the overall volunteer pool provides the bulk of the volunteer contribution. Luffman and Cromie (2003) noted that among arts and culture organisations in Canada: 'a core group of culture volunteers contributed almost three quarters of the total volunteer hours for culture organisations.'

Keaveney et al (1991) summed up this entire situation with their insightful comment: 'Ex-volunteers will attest that demands increase proportionally with a volunteer's willingness to comply.'

At times these demands do not even have to be voiced, as volunteers' high motivational levels lead them to seek additional work on their own, with the silent compliance of paid staff – a phenomenon known as 'exploitation through expectation'.

The causes of volunteer burnout

Preventing burnout from happening in the first place is thus a very desirable goal. We now go on to look at some of the common causes of burnout that relate to volunteer management and what can be done to minimise them.

People get burnt out when what they are doing is no longer exciting or interesting

People rarely feel burnt out when they are in the process of pursuing a goal that they find compelling or exciting. When burnout strikes, it is usually when the task seems like a chore we have to struggle through. This often happens when we lose sight of the purpose of our activities.

The degree to which a volunteer activity has intrinsic interest varies greatly from assignment to assignment. Some volunteer experiences provide volunteers with an activity that has the potential for high drama. Even in these cases, however, it is possible for volunteers to struggle with bureaucratic tussles, completing reports or the process of advocacy. When volunteers in a hospice, for example, focus on feeding patients, interviewing family members and attending meetings, they can lose sight of the fact that the position is to make sure that the last days of a patient are as rich as possible.

By keeping volunteers focused on this ultimate goal, members of staff invest the position with meaning. When talking to volunteers about their work, it can be mentioned in the context of the mission of the charity and the goals they are pursing. Volunteers in a friendly visitor programme, for example, might be asked, 'How are you doing in helping your client feel cared about and feel better about life?'

People get burnt out when their expectations do not match their reality

Some individuals begin volunteering with high expectations of accomplishment – 'I will change the world,' or 'I will significantly improve the life of a child.' Often these expectations can be met. Sometimes, however, there is a disparity between the expectations and the reality experienced by the volunteer. In some cases, this disparity can create frustration, a sense of failure and eventual burnout, especially if volunteers feel responsible for the perceived 'failure' to meet their expectations. Countering this tendency can be done through adjusting the expectation early in the volunteer experience (such as during the initial induction or training) to match more closely a reasonable and realistic expectation of accomplishment.

This condition can either develop over time or can occur suddenly in a traumatic situation for which volunteers discover they are not as prepared as they thought, as noted by the Federal Emergency Management Agency in the case of Emergency Medical Services (EMS) volunteers (FEMA, 1995):

> If the EMS organization fails to provide volunteers with sufficient notice as to the difficult situations EMTs [emergency medical technicians] may face, the

unanticipated emotional trauma of an emergency run with an unsatisfactory result may lead to the volunteer's subsequent failure to show up for calls or even to resignation.

People get burnt out when they feel they are facing an overwhelming burden

Some volunteer assignments are more complicated or more intense than others. Volunteers who have a complex or emotionally difficult task can feel that it is simply too much for them to accomplish. Volunteers who have a task that they do not understand may also view it as insurmountable, with the ambiguity of the task giving the volunteer the feeling that they do not know how to proceed.

Volunteers may also feel overwhelmed when time demands of volunteering come into conflict with other parts of their lives. Volunteers feel responsible as the escalating time demands seem insurmountable – either they must 'fail' in their volunteer effort or 'fail' in another part of their life. Not wishing to let the organisation down, volunteers work and work until they collapse.

People get burnt out when they do not feel supported

Volunteers must feel that staff will support their efforts. This is particularly important when volunteers work alone and in isolation from staff. To succeed in such assignments, they need to be self-directed, making their own decisions about what to do each day. Sometimes, this sense of being on one's own can be interpreted as being uncared for or unvalued.

Volunteers are giving us some of their precious leisure time. If they do not feel that the organisation values it, they will tend to drop out. Volunteers who work on their own are more prone to feeling unappreciated than volunteers who work in an office where there are many natural opportunities for staff to say thank you. However, even in those situations, staff will sometimes ignore volunteers.

Each volunteer needs to have a clearly identified supervisor who makes regular contact with the volunteer. This has many advantages beyond just giving the volunteer the feeling of being supported. One is that staff may discover, as they chat with volunteers about their progress, that a volunteer is doing something wrong. Another is that, knowing such a scheduled chat is coming up, volunteers will be given the incentive to make sure they have something positive to report. If they are procrastinating, the natural desire to avoid embarrassment encourages them to make progress for the benefit of the organisation before they have their scheduled conversation with the staff member. Helping them to overcome procrastination in this way reduces the sense of the task being the overwhelming burden mentioned above.

People get burnt out when their tasks feel repetitive

Sometimes volunteers may need a change of pace. They often have other skills that can be helpful to a programme in ways other than the position they initially agreed to take. For example, a volunteer with public relations skills might help the programme by developing recruitment posters and brochures or writing public interest stories for the press. Volunteers with skills in computer programming might help the organisation by upgrading its website. Volunteers with office skills might join consultations on creating better office systems. Wise programme leaders will know enough about each volunteer to have a sense of what these skills might be.

Experienced volunteers may also undertake supervisory tasks to help relieve overworked volunteer supervisors. They might, for example, help out with regular contact with volunteers, thus helping those active volunteers to feel supported.

People may give the appearance of burnout when they do not feel connected.

As discussed previously, one of the major motivational needs of human beings is to feel a sense of belonging – a sense of being part of a relationship with others. These relationships help to guard against burnout. Byron and Curtis (2002) noted:

> Another important element in reducing burnout is the presence of a strong sense of community and social cohesion ... WPR [Western Port Region, Australia] respondents who said an important reason for them joining Landcare was the involvement of people they respected had significantly lower burnout on the personal accomplishment subscale.

We have mentioned many ways to make volunteers feel like insiders. In our previous discussion, the focus was on staff and volunteers being regarded as being equal partners. In addition, volunteers can be assisted in feeling a rapport with other volunteers. Special efforts may be necessary to bring volunteers together so that they can easily identify with the programme and form relationships with other volunteers. In-service training sessions, social gatherings and events for the clients of the charity are some of the ways in which this can be done.

One thing to watch out for at such gatherings, however, is those volunteers who stand around awkwardly, not making connections. They may see other volunteers having a wonderful time together but may not know anyone well enough to feel comfortable starting a conversation. Staff in such circumstances can play the role of the good host, introducing volunteers to each other and helping them to find subjects of common interest to discuss.

Having something to talk to others about is a fundamental condition for feelings of belonging. New volunteers need to be integrated quickly with the older volunteers and staff. When a new volunteer joins the programme, staff should tell the others some interesting facts about that person so that others can have topics of conversation with which to engage them.

While most burnout occurs over time, burnout can also develop quickly if volunteers are exposed to extreme stress. Stewart et al (2004) studied volunteers who responded to the crash of Swissair Flight 111, and discovered that 46% of them experienced Post-Traumatic Stress Disorder, resulting in increased alcohol use. White (2001) studied burnout and compassion fatigue among volunteers working at Ground Zero in New York City.

Signs of burnout

Burnout may manifest itself in a number of ways but is usually accompanied by noticeable changes in the demeanour and behaviour of the affected person. Some of the signs to watch for include:

Physical signs

- Increased fatigue
- Physical exhaustion
- Insomnia or sleeping more than usual
- Headaches

Psychological signs

- Rigidity/loss of flexibility
- Feelings of apathy
- Emotional exhaustion
- Low morale
- Sense of hopelessness or of over-confidence
- Anger or resentment
- Dehumanising of clients
- Inability to make decisions
- Feelings of failure
- Depression

Behavioural signs

- Poor job performance
- Withdrawal
- Absenteeism
- Loss of enthusiasm
- Lack of focus on work
- Increased incidence of complaints
- Workaholic tendencies

You will note that some of the above appear contradictory – 'absenteeism' and 'workaholic tendencies' for example in the behavioural signs. Either of these can occur, and sometimes both can occur in the same individual, depending on the nature of the volunteer. The key is to look for extreme changes from the 'normal' pattern of behaviour of the volunteer.

Assisting a burnt-out volunteer

By keeping in close contact with volunteers, staff will find out if they think that they can cope with the work. Volunteer managers should keep in touch with volunteers on at least a weekly basis, if possible (and in some programmes, where the ratio of supervisors to volunteers is greater than 1 to 30, this is a daunting task), so that the problem can be identified early.

Once staff have determined that a volunteer feels overwhelmed, they can take steps to make the volunteer feel more capable of dealing with the position. One step is to help the volunteer break the overwhelming task into a series of 'bite-sized' pieces, each of which is easily understandable. If volunteers are able to view their assignments as a series of many small steps, they feel more capable of managing.

Another step is to assign a second volunteer to help. Similarly, staff can decide to play a more active role in the particular task. When volunteers feel they have a partner, they feel less alone and less overwhelmed. Netting et al (2000) found reduced burnout when volunteer ombudsman programmes established formal policies that allowed volunteers to 'hand off' complex complaints to staff.

The simplest response to burnout is temporarily to remove affected volunteers from their current positions, thus relieving them from the stresses which foster burnout. We think of this as our 'Crop Rotation Theory of Volunteer Involvement'. Either give the volunteer a sabbatical or else find another volunteer position that does not replicate the stressful conditions which are fostering burnout. If possible, this position should be in conditions which do not resemble the previous volunteer position and that allow the volunteer to experience feelings of success and personal connection to others.

The AIDS Committee of Toronto uses the following volunteer policy as a way of implementing this strategy:

On leave

An on-leave volunteer is one who is in a program but on leave from active volunteering in that program.

Volunteers may go on leave for up to one year. This leave may be taken at the volunteer's discretion for any reason including bereavement, study, illness, stress and burnout.

Do not be surprised if you encounter resistance from volunteers when you suggest changes in their level of involvement. If a proportion of the volunteers' own ego is invested in what they are doing they will find it difficult to give it up. Be strict in reminding them that any change is ultimately for the good of the programme, and that once they are able to, you want them to return to work, more capable than ever.

One of the most tragic aspects of volunteer burnout is that it is most likely to strike among the most dedicated and motivated volunteers and that these volunteers are often unwilling or unable to recognise and report their condition, commonly out of a sense of duty and personal responsibility.

This requires volunteer programme managers to be attuned to the condition of volunteers and to be ready to take proactive steps even when the volunteer does not come to them to report a difficulty. The causes of burnout addressed above can then provide possible ways of bringing the volunteer back from psychological distress.

Nesbitt et al (1996) in a study of AIDS volunteers suggested that:

... in order to reduce grief, special attention should be paid to allowing volunteers freely to express problems with emotional overload and workload adjustments, and providing clear emotional support as a reward.

Fostering support or discussion groups of volunteers would be one way to provide a forum for these discussions. Volunteers could talk about their difficulties and also discuss ways to cope with their stress.

Breaux (1993) recommends a programme of psychosocial support for volunteers, including education support (to allow volunteers to be successful), social support (to foster a safe volunteer environment and allow team building, fellowship and nurturing) and psychological support (to empower volunteers to confront and process their emotions, fears, concerns, frustrations and grief so that stress and burnout can be minimised).

Yufe (1998) offers the following general suggestions for assisting volunteers with burnout:

1   Maintain close contact with all volunteers ... Encourage your volunteers to contact you as well.

2   Whenever you encounter a volunteer – on the phone, on the job, at a meeting – ask friendly but probing questions about his or her current situation. 'How's the assignment going?' or 'Anything new with your client (patient)?' or 'I know this is a difficult one – how are you doing?' or 'What are you doing to take care of yourself?'

3   Elicit feedback from staff, clients, patients, families and even other volunteers to provide you with a well-rounded view of how the volunteer is performing.

4   Be alert for signs or burnout and/or co-dependency. Urge all volunteers to learn how to set limits, recognise appropriate boundaries and feel okay saying 'no'.

Facing the inevitable in systemic burnout

Widespread burnout throughout a volunteer system may be a sign of a deeper dysfunction than an individual problem. It may indicate that the scope of the volunteer role has become insurmountable in a volunteer setting, requiring too much time or too much commitment to be sustained within a normal volunteer assignment. The requirements of the work may simply have 'outgrown' their ability to be provided by volunteers. This becomes a cascading process, since, as volunteers leave, additional work has to be assumed by those who stay. As Bussell and Forbes (2002) commented: 'In some instances, the decline in the numbers volunteering often means that the work is left to fewer people and this discourages volunteers from continuing.'

Phillips et al (2002) noted this effect among volunteer caregivers in Canada:

It is evident that the demand will not be met by squeezing more time out of existing care giving volunteers. These volunteers are already putting in long hours and, given their average age, will likely face significant health problems themselves in the near future.

Taylor (2004) reported that among key volunteers in sports clubs in England, 35% contributed 250 hours a year or more. Taylor et al also noted (2003) the impact of this trend combined with falling volunteer numbers:

> These considerations illustrate a dangerous downward spiral in that certain key volunteers expand the role they take, because of their own enthusiasm and expertise, or because they take over other roles because it is easier to do this than recruit new volunteers, or because they perceive it impossible to recruit new volunteers. The role to be replaced is then defined by what the existing or last post-holder did, rather than with reference to what the club actually needs. Thus it becomes even harder to find a replacement for individuals.

Byron and Curtis (2002) raised this issue in relation to burnout among Landcare volunteers in Australia:

> While it may appear justified to advocate higher levels of participation to manage burnout, the extent that any increase in activity would be sustainable appears questionable. Effective watershed groups are commonly associated with a small core of highly dedicated and motivated individuals. As the activity of watershed groups increases, these individuals are likely to become overloaded.

This syndrome may be alleviated by redesigning volunteer assignments to allow team or job-sharing arrangements but some systems may reach a point at which the volume of work required of a volunteer is simply beyond reasonable capacity to sustain. It is at this point that many previously all-volunteer organisations contemplate the move to paid staffing.

For a more complete examination of this, using the Australian Landcare volunteer effort as an example, see Curtis (2000) and Byron et al (2001) or Coleman (2002), who examined this phenomenon in UK cricket sports clubs, and also Nichols (2003), who looked at the effects of 'professionalisation' in English national governing sports bodies. A similar controversy occurred regarding volunteer firefighters in the US (see Perkins, 1990 and Thompson and Bono, 1993). Brunet et al (2001) noted in respect of this community that:

> ... it may be that there are some levels of fire protection that simply cannot be attained by volunteer departments. Especially in difficult environments, the amount of training required may be so great and the management of so many part-time volunteers so time-consuming that volunteers would have to devote themselves to their departments nearly full-time.

This is, obviously, a far greater problem than that created when individual volunteers suffer overload.

chapter 10

MOVING VOLUNTEERS FROM SHORT-TERM TO LONG-TERM COMMITMENTS

The shift to short-term volunteering

The trend in English-speaking countries is away from volunteers making long-term commitments. Instead, they are more likely to want a term of service, sometimes as short as one day, with a defined end-point. In a study by the JC Penny Company in 1987, 79% of non-volunteers cited 'short-term' assignments as the most important incentive for becoming volunteers.

A study in Canada (Handy and Srinivasan, 2003) found that 81% of volunteer managers reported an increase in short-term volunteers and 63% reported an increase of volunteers requesting an assignment of less than three months. In a companion study in 2004, Handy et al found that 80% of reporting hospitals had an increase in volunteers who served for three months to a year.

A survey by the National Volunteer and Philanthropy Centre of Singapore in 2002 found that: 'for the non-volunteers who are very likely/likely/may volunteer in the future, 29% prefer commitments of less than 3 months and another 20% prefer commitments of between 3 to 6 months.'

In a study of volunteers over the age of 45, the American Association of Retired Persons (AARP) (2003) found that 48% only volunteered from time to time, for a specific project or activity. A similar study of AARP members in Delaware (American Association of Retired Persons, 2001) found that 33% volunteered occasionally during the year for special projects, 28% volunteered for a regular time each month and, in addition, volunteered extra hours for special projects, and 19% usually spent about the same amount of time volunteering each month. Younger members (age 50–59) were more likely than older volunteers to volunteer occasionally during the year.

Greenberg (1997) found that 47% of potential volunteers in Alberta were unwilling to make a year-long commitment. Safrit (2001), in a study of young adults, found that both non-volunteers (56%) and current volunteers (45%) cited inability to make a long-term commitment among their reasons for not volunteering more.

Wollebaek and Selle (2003), in a study of Norwegian organisations, found that younger members volunteered at the same rate as older members but did so in a different manner: 'The new model of participation is therefore characterized by a strong activity orientation, short-term commitment, extensive turnover and a weak or contained value basis.'

Volunteer Development Scotland (2003) reported that 21% of the Scottish population said they would be more likely to volunteer if they were sure that volunteering would fit in among all their other commitments.

Lasby (2004), in a study of Canadian volunteers, found the following pattern of those citing 'no year-round commitment' as a requirement for volunteering:

Age	%
• 15–24	24
• 25–34	47
• 35–44	50
• 45–54	48
• 55–64	43
• 65+	41

A 2002 study of young adults by Lake Snell Perry & Associates found that episodic volunteering was popular among young adults with children – with 30% volunteering every month and 10% volunteering every week. Lopez (2004), analysing a US survey of 16–25 year-olds, found that while 40.3% reported volunteering, 'just over half, 22.2 percent [of those who volunteered], volunteered regularly, suggesting that they engage in episodic volunteering more often than their older counterparts.'

Overall, in the US, Independent Sector's research (2000) reported: '41% volunteered sporadically, 39% volunteered at a regularly scheduled time, and 9% volunteered only for special occasions.' In Canada, McClintock (2004), based on the 2000 National Survey of Giving, Volunteering and Participating, reported: 'One barrier was constant among non-volunteers in all age, income, and employment status groups: unwillingness to make a year-round commitment.' A 2003 survey by the Points of Light Foundation (Cihlar, 2004) found that its constituent groups rated: 'More people interested in short/episodic opportunities' as the number-one trend facing volunteering.

This trend towards involvement in a shorter timeframe is simply part of an overall trend in modern life. Macduff (2005), summing up considerable data on episodic volunteering, concluded:

> The post-modern era is characterized by ambiguity and precariousness in life. People who thought they would work for the same company for life are laid off

and, in some cases, lose pension benefits. Children do not join the same groups to which their parents and grandparents belonged, and often move thousands of miles from the home of their birth to create a new life biography. The 21st century has the individual as the solo artist, creating his or her own experiences, and this performance includes the selection of the style of volunteering.

Accommodating short-term volunteering within traditional volunteer management

Recruiting volunteers for a short-term event is a relatively commonplace and relatively easy practice these days. On practically any given weekend there is a variety of available volunteer activities that basically require the commitment of a few hours, often spent with friends, ranging from building houses, to cleaning up parks, to the various 'a-thons' that permeate the landscape. There are even volunteer organisations that specialise in organising these activities and targeting recruitment to those interested in short-term volunteering.

The only problem, of course, is that operating a sustained volunteer effort on the basis of these one-off events is a difficult, if not impossible, task. Most organisations need volunteers who are actively involved more often than once a year and who are willing to come back once the fun event is over to do the hard work that really needs to be done. In particular, they need volunteers who are willing to accept responsibility and perform leadership functions.

Fraser and Gottlieb (2001) noted the difficulty faced by many organisations in accomplishing this:

> The point seems to be that any volunteer work requiring a long-term commitment to administrative responsibilities, practical chores, or any activities other than direct contact with clients seems to be shunned by volunteers, perhaps because the work has a job-like character and perhaps because the rewards are not as direct and palpable as direct client service.

This seemingly lackadaisical attitude of volunteers is often not appreciated by paid staff. Li-Kook (2002), writing about the Puppet Festival Chunchon in Korea that involves short-term volunteers, found different attitudes about how long volunteers should work:

> The staff members' attitudes were expressed in the comment, 'volunteers' hard working is beautiful' and, to some extent, in the tendency to take for granted volunteers overworking. The distinct attitudes toward work tended to

cause conflicts between the paid staff and the volunteers. Volunteers complained about being frequently overworked. One of the key informants stated, 'I am not their servant. Why did they break their promise – 8 hours per day?' One of the staff members said, 'They work only for five days. If they decided to help this festival, I think, they could work a little more. '

The most common reason given for not wishing to make a long-term commitment is 'I don't have time.' In many cases, this is simply a polite way of expressing the following substantive concerns:

- Is what I will get out of donating the time worth the time it will take?
- How much hassle will be involved?
- Can I trust that you'll deliver what you promise?

These are difficult questions to answer effectively when the volunteer has no existing relationship with you and thus little reason to believe your answers.

Developing a system for encouraging incremental commitment

Here are some tips for approaching this situation. We are warning you that they require a planned and organised effort and that you will have to invest a lot of work before you earn your reward. Nonetheless, we think you will find it well worth your time. Ours is a three-step process to the successful recruitment of the volunteers that you really need, not just the ones who show up to get the free T-shirt.

Organise attractor events and positions

An attractor event is designed to engage the attention and short-term involvement of larger numbers of volunteers. Large events are perfect for encouraging previously uninvolved people to consider volunteering. As an example of their effectiveness, UK Sport (2002), in an evaluation of the XVII Commonwealth Games, discovered that 24% of those who came forward to volunteer had no previous volunteer experience whatsoever but were attracted by the size, scope, timeframe and excitement of the event.

Attractor events can be organised around a clean-up (park, home, non-profit agency), around community education (a shopping centre display or a corporate fair), an 'a-thon' fundraiser, an educational or outreach event or any other activity which meets the following requirements:

- It can involve large numbers of people in a variety of volunteer tasks and projects.

- The volunteer positions do not require any substantial training or preparation.
- The work is fun and exciting and allows people to work with others.
- The activity is photogenic, thus attracting attention.

The event itself should also accomplish something worthwhile, although this is not the primary aim. In addition, the event should allow all those who participate (volunteers and the general public) to gain an introduction to the cause, clientele and operation of your agency, with contributions made by volunteers to the organisation's work particularly highlighted. This introduction can be provided via printed matter, demonstrations, or whatever method seems to work in your setting. The key is that current volunteers should be a prominent part of the event. These volunteers should be encouraged to tell the new participants about the other types of volunteering roles they are participating in with the charity.

Attractor positions can also accomplish the desired goal of encouraging prospective volunteers to 'test the waters' in the organisation. Designing good attractor positions can be viewed as similar to developing assignments that might be handled by a consultant. They should have the following characteristics:

- They have a definite goal or result in mind, often a definite product.
- They have a defined timeframe, usually fairly short.
- They may require a particular expertise or ability.
- They can be 'owned' by the volunteer, in the sense that the responsibility for accomplishment will be clearly bestowed on the volunteer.
- It will be clear whether the work is done successfully or not.
- They should directly relate in some way to the talents of the volunteers or to a group or activity that the volunteer cares about.

The key phrases to remember in developing these events are 'hands-on', 'fun', and 'immediate gratification'.

In addition, identifying these short-term volunteer opportunities differently may help to reassure people who are worried about over-commitment. Some popular phrases include:

- 'day of' volunteers
- 'just in time' volunteers
- 'flexitime' volunteers
- 'drop-in' volunteers
- 'episodic' volunteers
- 'one-time' volunteers
- 'à la carte' volunteers
- 'done-in-a-day' volunteers
- 'one-off' volunteers.

For more extensive volunteer opportunities that are not event-based but are still time-limited you might try referring to the work as a 'consulting project' rather than a 'position'. The difference in terminology can generate a different response.

All of these are intended to make the prospective volunteer more likely to take the test drive; to try volunteering with an organisation with which they are not already familiar.

Scout for the more engaged

During the event, current volunteers should be assigned to work with groups of newcomers. These volunteers are in addition to those mentioned above who will also participate by telling their stories. These 'scout' volunteers should be recruited for the part and one of them may provide oversight for several teams or work areas. Part of their assignment is to help manage the work to be done during the event, although another part of their assignment involves 'scouting' those who are attending, looking for those who show the most interest and potential.

These scouts should be encouraged to:

- establish personal contact with each of the volunteers with whom they are working
- give the newcomers a sense of 'welcome' and appreciation
- get the names and contact information of those attending, so that they can be thanked afterwards
- ensure that each new volunteer receives some basic information about the agency and about its involvement with volunteers, and receives a briefing on the cause of the organisation and its work in furthering that cause.

Particular elements to look for in volunteers with a potential for further development are those who:

- are having lots of fun
- seem to like organising others
- indicate interest in the cause
- seem to have some personal connection to the cause.

Special attention should be paid to locating those who are 'in charge' of already-established groups of volunteers (such as workplace teams, school groups, social clubs and the like), since they are likely to be personality types who enjoy being leaders and doing additional work.

As an example of this approach, the Burning Man festival in Nevada appoints volunteer coordinators, who are assigned to the specific teams that run various activities at the event. These coordinators take responsibility for welcoming and placing volunteers who come to their team area, ensuring that those who enrol either before or during the event are effectively integrated into the team structure. These coordinators are different from the overall volunteer management team that oversees and plans the entire volunteer system for the event. In 2001 there were 50 volunteer coordinators; in 2002 there were 75. They were needed to try to provide direct contact with the more than 3,000 volunteers who are on site at Burning Man. For more on this, see the Afterburn Report 2001 at http://after-burn.burningman.com/01/community/volunteers.html.

And for general amusement, go to the Afterburn Report 2002 (http://after-burn.burningman.com/02/community/volunteer.html) and click on 'About this photo' in the middle of the page: you will see what life as a volunteer coordinator can be like if you are having a really good time.

Scouts should make notes about those they think have the potential for development and a debriefing should be held following the event. The debriefing should cover who might be receptive to further involvement, what types of volunteering roles they have shown interest in and how best they might be drawn further into the organisation.

If the context of the work is not in a group event, then whoever is supervising the work of the volunteer should perform the functions mentioned above.

Connecting nurturing with recognition

You can also tie the nurturing process into the volunteer recognition system. The Girl Scouts, Central Savannah River Council, for example, utilises a system that divides volunteers into two categories – episodic and progressive – and then matches awards to increased participation, as you will see in the following chart:

Award	Criteria	Recognition
Episodic		
Community Participation	• A one-time or one-day service to the troop/group, service unit, council or GSUSA • Completed required learning experiences	Thank-you letter
Citizenship in Girl Scouting	• Returns for a second or third round of service • Provides support through two or three short-term assignments for the troop/group, service unit, council or GSUSA	Certificate

Social Responsibility in Girl Scouting	• Provides fourth round of service to the troop/group, service unit, council or GSUSA	Volunteer service pin

Progressive

The Girl Scout Volunteer Achievement Award	• First successful volunteer service completion on a board committee or • First successful volunteer service completion on a task group assignment, or • First experience or troop or group leadership, or • First service experience of service unit management, or • Successful service to GSUSA for one year, and • Completed required training. Appointed and agreed to serve for another year	Volunteer development pin with chain
The Girl Scout Mentoring Award	• Served as coach or mentor for a new volunteer, or • Provided ongoing support resulting in retention of new volunteer, and • Mentor nominated by protégé.	White key on adult development pin
The Girl Scout Volunteer Executive Award	• Council or national level leadership role • Made significant contributions	Black key on adult development pin

Nurture additional involvement

The process of cultivating those whose potential has been identified will vary depending upon your circumstances, but here are some possible avenues to explore:

1   If the event is a recurring one, you can increase involvement by offering additional work within the context of the event. This might include asking the volunteer to provide feedback about the event, offering them a promotion within the activity or group with whom they served in the past year or asking them to participate in helping to organise and operate a forthcoming event. This invitation should be offered by the scout volunteer who has developed a personal relationship with the newcomer and it should be based upon being impressed with the quality of the work done by the volunteer. The offer should be phrased in terms of being a continuation of the work that has already been done rather than as an entirely new task or activity.

2   The volunteer should receive some sign of promotion with the agency, such as an official title which indicates their new status, access to materials or equipment, a business card or some other item which creates an official link with the organisation. They should also be provided with 'insider' information

not available to other volunteers who merely work at events. As McCune and Nelson (1995) commented: 'A promotion on the job shows appreciation for abilities. So an increase in responsibilities and supervision of others via an upgrade in title acknowledges a volunteer's outstanding work.'

3   While volunteers are doing additional work on the event, they should receive further details about the agency and its work. This should include information about the work of the agency and about the variety of volunteer positions that are available within it. Some of this information should be things which are not generally known, since this will give the volunteer a sense that they are receiving inside information about the organisation and its work; information not generally available to others.

4   The types of volunteering roles available should represent an ascending scale of complexity and responsibility. They should include short and easy tasks, and then have a staircase of more difficult roles. One way to accomplish this is to have the volunteer assist other volunteers in 'higher' positions. The volunteer should be exposed to current volunteers in these positions, who are given an opportunity to talk about their work and why they enjoy it. These discussions will serve as a low-pressure recruitment effort. From time to time these current volunteers can increase the pressure by asking the potential volunteer to 'help them out' on something they are working on. This should be something that will give the potential volunteer exposure to what the volunteers are doing without requiring a big commitment.

5   Volunteers should have latitude in selecting the type of volunteering roles they want to do. This element of 'choice' is of critical importance in fostering interest in additional volunteering (Stukas et al, 1999, and Clary and Snyder, 1999). It helps greatly, by the way, to have a wide variety of volunteer roles available, since offering options increases your chance of resonating with the potential volunteer.

6   The potential volunteer should also be introduced to staff and volunteers at the agency. Becoming friends with others in the organisation can serve as an anchor that holds the connection of the volunteer to the agency.

7   While this exposure process is occurring, further scouting of the interests and reactions of the potential volunteer should be undertaken. This scouting should fine-tune the effort to discover the type of motivation and possible volunteer role that would be most appealing to the potential volunteer.

Developing career ladders for volunteers

'Career ladders' are organised systems to encourage and assist volunteers in progressing through different levels of work and responsibility within a volunteer system.

The American National Red Cross has worked extensively to develop career ladders for volunteers, with many possible paths of advancement available. It noted of its own system (1988):

> Due to the complexity and diversity of the Red Cross, interested and qualified volunteers have a number of possible career paths available to them. At the chapter level, for example, a service volunteer can progress to becoming the service chairman, chairman of volunteers, a member of the board and, finally, chapter chairman. Within a service, a volunteer can also move upward. An instructor can become an instructor trainer and a trainer of instructor trainers. A disaster volunteer can add a variety of skills to his/her disaster service proficiencies, including disaster operation management. At the top of that ladder is becoming a member of the national disaster force and a disaster manager on national disaster operations.

It significantly, however, does not attempt to force volunteers to accept ever more responsibility in order to progress:

> The Red Cross has recently been stressing that 'up is not the only way' and that career development can and often should involve moves that are other than vertical.

Thinking differently about volunteer involvement

For many organisations, volunteer involvement has been treated as an 'either/or' proposition. Individuals were either in the system or not in the system. The new reality of volunteer involvement is a little more complex – volunteers may display various levels of commitment and involvement, moving in and out of the system and participating in different ways at different times. Organisations wanting increased levels of involvement have to work to persuade and groom volunteers for greater levels of participation.

The theory behind the process outlined above is relatively simple:

- People are more likely to 'test the waters' if offered small commitments.
- People will proceed at their own speed through the levels of involvement; some will stop along the way.
- When properly nurtured and cultivated, some people will keep progressing up the levels.

- When you attempt to force people into too much, too soon, they will resolve the problem by leaving.

The model described in this chapter is similar to one proposed by Gaskin (2003), which suggested the following stages of involvement:

- The **doubter** is outside volunteering, and may have attitudes, characteristics or circumstances that keep them a non-volunteer.
- The **starter** has entered volunteering by making an enquiry or application.
- The **doer** has committed themselves to being a volunteer and begun volunteering.
- The **stayer** persists as a long-term volunteer.

Hustinx (2004), in a study of volunteers with the Flemish Red Cross, discovered the following patterns of styles of volunteering:

1 **Episodic contributors**: those who volunteered only one or two times during the year, but who often continued volunteering over the course of several years on a recurrent basis (23% had been involved for more than 10 years). These volunteers typically were involved in providing project or programme assistance.
2 **Established administrators**: those who volunteered on a regular basis, usually in a formal office with specialised job responsibilities.
3 **Reliable co-workers**: those involved on a fairly stable, regular and time-consuming basis, usually in assisting staff with activities.
4 **Service-oriented core volunteers**: who participated on a regular basis, spending a significant amount of time, and were typically involved both in service provision and administrative tasks. Many of these volunteers were relatively new, with 65% having been involved for less than five years.
5 **Critical key figures**: those involved on an intense basis with critical leadership tasks and fundraising. Over 80% of them had been Red Cross volunteers for more than five years.

Within this pattern of styles, some volunteers tended to remain within a single style and others changed style over the years, typically by moving to higher levels of responsibility.

Potential dangers

As in any process, some mistakes are easy to make. Here are some things to avoid:

- **Getting too greedy, too fast**
  Offering volunteers more than they seem to want to do can be a fatal mistake. The trick, as in fishing, is to make the volunteers want to take the bait, not to

force it upon them. Remember that, unlike fishing, the volunteer can always get off the hook.

■ **Relying on make-work assignments**

The early steps of this process can only succeed if the initial jobs offered to the volunteer are short-term and productive. If volunteers think at any stage that their time is being wasted, you have lost the battle. All of the assignments on the 'career ladder' must be meaningful ones and volunteers must be able to stop at any point in the process and feel good about the work they are doing.

■ **Having an opportunity for true advancement**

The implicit offer in this process is that the volunteer can become a real leader in your organisation. This is, of course, only true if your organisation has upward mobility for volunteers and if the current leaders are willing to step aside as new talent emerges. If your current volunteer structure is petrified, it will be very difficult to get new blood into the system.

Organisations are more likely to talk about the need to provide promotional opportunities for volunteers than actually to do something about it. In a study of national health organisations in 1996, the Points of Light Foundation found that:

> While providing opportunities for volunteers to hold leadership positions was considered one of the most important current issues facing VHAs [Voluntary Health Agencies], only 21% of the VHAs reported they fully implemented explicit 'career ladders'. Furthermore, only 17% of the agencies reported they collect data on the number of volunteers promoted into more responsible roles.

The procedure described above may seem cumbersome, but it is recognition that few people will devote their time and lives to something on first contact. It is, however, possible to nurture and develop volunteer talent if you are willing to devote time, energy and attention to getting to know the volunteers, determining what would best gain their interest and then working with them to develop their involvement. DeMarco (1998), in a study of current volunteers in Ontario, determined that: 'Many past [volunteer] activities were project based or time limited. These were "test runs" which allowed for a taste of volunteering within a limited commitment and likely paved the way for their current more serious commitment.'

USEFUL ADDRESSES

Business in the Community (BITC)

137 Shepherdess Walk, London N1 7RQ
Tel: 020 7566 8650, e-mail: information@bitc.org.uk
website: www.bitc.org.uk

Community Service Volunteers (CSV)

237 Pentonville Road, London N1 9NJ
Tel: 020 7278 6601, email: information@cvs.org.uk
website: www.csv.org.uk

Directory of Social Change

24 Stephenson Way, London NW1 2DP
Tel: 08450 77 77 07, website: www.dsc.org.uk

do-it

First Floor, 50 Featherstone Street, London EC1Y 8RT
Tel: 020 7250 5700, e-mail: info@do-it.org.uk
website: www.do-it.org.uk

Media Trust

2nd Floor, Riverwalk House, 157–161 Millbank, London SW1P 4RR
Tel: 020 7217 3717, e-mail: info@mediatrust.org
website: www.mediatrust.org

Millennium Volunteers

England: http://vinspired.com/
Wales: www.wcva.org.uk/volunteering/
Northern Ireland: http://www.volunteering-ni.org/what_we__do/
millennium_volunteers/

National Association for Voluntary Community Action (NAVCA)

The Tower, 2 Furnival Square, Sheffield S1 4QL
Tel: 0114 278 6636, e-mail: navca@navca.org.uk
website: www.navca.org.uk

National Council for Ethnic Minority Voluntary Sector Organisations (CEMVO)

Boardman House, 64 Broadway, Stratford, London E15 1NG
Tel: 0800 652 0391/020 8432 0000, e-mail: enquiries@emf-cemvo.co.uk
website: www.emf-cemvo.co.uk

Mercy Corps

website: www.mercycorps.org

Northern Ireland Volunteer Development Agency

129 Ormeau Road, Belfast BT7 1SH
Tel: 028 9023 6100, e-mail: info@volunteernow.co.uk
website: www.volunteering-ni.org

Prohelp

Business in the Community, 137 Shepherdess Walk, London N1 7RQ
Tel: 020 7566 8650
e-mail: information@bitc.org.uk
website: www.prohelp.org.uk

REACH

89 Albert Embankment, London SE1 7TP
Tel: 020 7582 6543, e-mail: mail@reach-online.org.uk
website: www.volwork.org.uk

Volunteer Development Scotland

Jubilee House, Forthside Way, Stirling FK8 1QZ
Tel: 01786 479593, e-mail: vds@vds.org.uk
website: www.vds.org.uk

Volunteering England

Regent's Wharf, 8 All Saints Street, London N1 9RL

New Oxford House, 16 Waterloo Street, Birmingham B2 5UG
Tel: 0845 305 6979, e-mail: volunteering@volunteering.org.uk
website: www.volunteering.org.uk

TimeBank

2nd Floor, Downstream Building, 1 London Bridge, London SE1 9BG
Tel: 0845 456 1668
website: www.timebank.org.uk

VolunQueer

Kairos in Soho, Unit 1, 10-11 Archer Street, Soho, London W1D 7AX
Tel: 020 7437 6063, e-mail: info@kairosinsoho.org.uk
website: www.kairosinsoho.org.uk/volunqueer

Wales Council for Voluntary Action

Baltic House, Mount Stuart Square, Cardiff Bay, Cardiff CF10 5FH
Tel: 0870 607 1666, e-mail: help@wcva.org.uk
website: www.wcva.org.uk

Youth Action Network

Crest House, 7 Highfield Road, Edgbaston, Birmingham B15 3ED
Tel: 0121 455 9732, e-mail: info@youthactionnetwork.org.uk
website: www.youthactionnetwork.org.uk

FURTHER READING

The Directory of Social Change (DSC) is an independent voice for positive social change, set up in 1975 to help volunteer organisations become more effective. It does this by providing practical, challenging and affordable information and training to meet the current, emerging and future needs of the sector. The following titles are available from DSC. Telephone 08450 77 77 07 or e-mail publications@dsc.org.uk for a complete catalogue, or visit the DSC website: www.dsc.org.uk.

Editions were correct at the time of going to press but may be subject to change.

Essential Volunteer Management, Steve McCurley & Rick Lynch, DSC, 2nd edition, 1998. Reprinted with updates 2007

The Good Practice Guide: for everyone who works with volunteers, Volunteering England, 2nd edition, 2002

Recruiting Volunteers, Fraser Dyer & Ursula Jost, DSC, 2002. Reprinted with updates 2010

The Russell-Cooke Voluntary Sector Legal Handbook, James Sinclair Taylor and the Charity Team at Russell-Cooke Solicitors, Editor Sandy Adirondack, DSC, 3rd edition, 2009

BIBLIOGRAPHY

Aitken, Allen, 'Identifying Key Issues Affecting the Retention of Emergency Service Volunteers', *Australian Journal of Emergency Management*, winter 2000, www.ema. gov.au/5virtuallibrary/pdfs/vol15no2/aitken.pdf.

Aldridge, Martin, *The Way Ahead: Development of Effective Recruitment* and *Retention Strategies for Volunteer Fire Services*, Fire and Emergency Services Authority of Western Australia, 2003, www.germanfiredept.org/Australian VolunteerStudy.pdf.

Amenta, MM, 'Death, Anxiety, Purpose in Life and Duration of Service in Hospice Volunteers', *Psychological Reports*, June 1984.

American Association of Retired Persons, *AARP 2001 Delaware Member Survey: Volunteerism*, Washington: AARP, 2001.

American Association of Retired Persons, *AARP South Dakota Member Survey: Volunteerism*, Washington: AARP, 2004.

American Association of Retired Persons, *Time and Money: An In-depth Look at 45+ Volunteers and Donors*, Washington: AARP, 2003.

American National Red Cross, *Volunteer 2000 Study: The Resource Document*, Washington: American National Red Cross, 1988.

Ancans, Indra, *Why People Volunteer*, Ottawa: Volunteer Centre of Ottawa-Carleton, 1992.

Australian Bureau of Statistics, 'Voluntary Work, Australia', Catalogue 4441.0, Canberra: Australian Government Publishing Service, 1995.

Australian Bureau of Statistics, 'Voluntary Work, Australia', June 2001, www.abs.gov.au/ausstats.

Bakatsa, Maria and Stephen Lea, *Measuring Job Satisfaction in Voluntary Workers: Effects of Age and Motivation*, www.ex.ac.uk/~SEGLea/results/volunteers.html.

Balliette, John and Marilyn Goad Smith, 'Empowering Volunteers through Involvement,' *Journal of Extension*, fall 1990.

Bell, Karen, *Assessing the Benefits for Conservation of Volunteer Involvement in Conservation Activities*, Wellington, New Zealand Department of Conservation, 2003.

Bennett, L, MW Ross and R Sunderland, 'The Relationship between Recognition, Rewards and Burnout in AIDS Caring', *AIDS Care*, April 1996.

Black, Beverly and Diana DiNitto, 'Volunteers Who Work with Survivors of Rape and Battering: Motivations, Acceptance, Satisfaction, Length of Service and Gender Differences', *Journal of Social Science Research*, Vol. 20(1/2) 1994.

Black, Beverly and Pam Kovacs, 'Direct Care and Nondirect Care Hospice Volunteers: Motivations, Acceptance, Satisfaction and Length of Service', *Journal of Volunteer Administration*, winter 1996.

Black, Beverly and Pam Kovacs, 'Age-Related Variation in Roles Performed by Hospice Volunteers', *Journal of Applied Gerontology*, December 1999.

Boraas, Stephanie, 'Volunteerism in the United States', *Monthly Labor Review*, June 2003.

Breaux, Tommy, 'Psychosocial Support: A Crucial Component for the Successful Management of AIDS Volunteers', *Journal of Volunteer Administration*, fall/winter 1993/94.

Brown, Eleanor and Jan Zahrly, 'Nonmonetary Rewards for Skilled Volunteer Labor: A Look at Crisis Intervention Volunteers', *Nonprofit and Voluntary Sector Quarterly*, summer 1989.

Brown, Kathleen, 'Thoughts on Supervision of Volunteers', *Voluntary Action Leadership*, spring 1984.

Brudney, Jeffrey, *Fostering Volunteer Programs in the Public Sector*, San Francisco: Jossey-Bass, 1990.

Brudney, Jeffrey and Beth Gazley, 'The USA Freedom Corps and the Role of the States', *Spectrum: The Journal of State Government*, fall 2002.

Brunet, Alexia, Larry DeBoer and Kevin McNamara, 'Community Choice between Volunteer and Professional Fire Departments', *Nonprofit and Voluntary Sector Quarterly*, March 2001.

Bryant, RA and AG Harvey, 'Posttraumatic Stress Reactions in Volunteer Firefighters', *Journal of Trauma and Stress*, January 1996.

Bureau of Labor Statistics, *Volunteering in the United States 2003*, Washington: Department of Labor, 2003, www.bls.gov/news.release/volun.nr0.htm.

Bussell, Helen and Deborah Forbes, 'Understanding the Volunteer Market: the What, Where, Who and Why of Volunteering', *International Journal of Nonprofit and Voluntary Sector Marketing*, Vol. 7(3) 2002.

Byrne, Richard and Faye Caskey, 'For Love or Money? What Motivates Volunteers', *Journal of Extension*, fall 1985, www.joe.org/joe/1985fall/sa1.html.

Byron, Ian and Allan Curtis, 'Landcare in Australia: Burnout Out and Browned Off', *Local Environment*, August 2001.

Byron, Ian and Allan Curtis, 'Maintaining Volunteer Commitment to Local Watershed Initiatives', *Environmental Management*, July 2002.

Bryon, Ian, Allan Curtis and Michael Lockwood, 'Exploring Burnout in Australia's Landcare Program: A Case Study in the Shepparton Region', *Society and Natural Resources*, December 2001.

Campbell, Katherine, *Powerful Volunteer Connections: A Toolkit for Maximizing Your Organization's Volunteer Resources*, Washington: Points of Light Foundation, 2004.

Canadian Museums Association, *More than Willing Hands: Report on Voluntarism*, 2001, www.museums.ca/cma1/whatsnew/Issues/volunteers/voluntarismreport.htm.

Capner, M and ML Caltabiano, 'Factors affecting the Progression towards Burnout: A Comparison of Professional and Volunteer Counselors', *Psychological Report*, 73, 1993.

Catano, Victor, Morgan Pond and E Kevin Kelloway, 'Exploring Commitment and Leadership in Volunteer Organizations', *Leadership and Organization Development*, Vol. 22(6) 2001.

Cessford, C and G Marley, 'Factors that Influence Retention and Attrition amongst Volunteer Community First Responders within the North East Ambulance Service NHS Trust, First Responders within the North East Ambulance Service NHS Trust', *Emergency Medical Journal*, January 2003.

Cheng, Cliff, 'Uniform Change: An Ethnography on Organizational Symbolism, Volunteer Motivation and Dysfunctional Change in a Paramilitary Organization', *Leadership & Organization Development Journal*, January/February 1998.

Chevrier, Fiona, Roxanne Steuer and Jackie MacKenzie, 'Factors Affecting Satisfaction among Community-Based Hospice Volunteer Visitors', *American Journal of Hospice and Palliative Care*, July/August 1994.

Cihlar, Christopher, *A Friendly Atmosphere for Your Volunteers*, Washington: Points of Light Foundation, 2004.

Cihlar, Christopher, *Points of Light Foundation Strategic Plan: Constituent Survey and Data Analysis & 2003 National Conference Focus Group Input*, Washington: Points of Light Foundation, 2004.

CIS Research Centre, *Assessing Capacity to Support Volunteerism*, Edmonton: Volunteer Alberta, 2004.

Clark, Dawne and Rena Shimoni, *Recruiting, Retaining and Supporting Volunteers for Long-Term Social Change*, Toronto: Canadian Centre for Philanthropy, 2002a.

Clark, Dawne and Rena Shimoni, *Volunteerism and Social Change: A Case Study of the Calgary Children's Initiative*, Toronto: Canadian Centre for Philanthropy, 2002b.

Clark, Sherry, *You Cannot be Serious! A Guide to Involving Volunteers with Mental Health Problems*, National Centre for Volunteering, 2003.

Clary, Gil and Mark Snyder, 'A Functional Analysis of Altruism and Prosocial Behavior: the Case of Volunteerism', in Margaret Clark (ed.) *Prosocial Behavior*, California: Sage Publications, 1991.

Clary, Gil and Mark Snyder, 'The Motivations to Volunteer: Theoretical and Practical Considerations', *Current Directions in Psychological Science*, October 1999.

Clary, Gil, Mark Snyder and Robert Ridge, 'Volunteers' Motivations: A Functional Strategy for the Recruitment, Placement and Retention of Volunteers', *Nonprofit Management and Leadership*, summer 1992.

Clary, EG, Mark Snyder, Robert Ridge, John Copeland, Arthur Stukas, Julie Haugen and Peter Miene, 'Understanding and Assessing the Motivations of Volunteers: A Functional Approach', *Journal of Personality and Social Psychology*, June 1998.

Claxton, RPR, J Catalan and AP Burgess, 'Psychological Distress and Burnout among Buddies: Demographic, Situational and Motivational Factors', *AIDS Care*, April 1998.

Coleman, Richard, 'Characteristics of Volunteering in UK Sport: Lessons from Cricket', *Managing Leisure*, October 2002.

Colomy, Paul, Huey-tsuh Chen and Gregg Andrews, 'Situational Facilities and Volunteer Work', *Journal of Volunteer Administration*, winter 1987/88.

Community Literacy of Ontario, 'Economic Value of Volunteer Involvement in Community Literacy Agencies in Ontario', 1997, www.nald.ca/PROVINCE/ONT/volman/economic/value.htm.

Cook, Ann, 'Retiring the Volunteer: Facing Reality when Service is No Longer Possible', *Journal of Volunteer Administration*, summer 1992.

Cox, E, 'Rewarding Volunteers: A Study of Participant Responses to the Assessment and Accreditation of Volunteer Learning', *Studies in the Education of Adults*, October 2002.

Coyne, BS, and EJ Coyne, 'Getting, Keeping and Caring for Unpaid Volunteers for Professional Golf Tournaments', *Human Resource Development International*, June 2001.

Cravens, Jayne, 'What Are Your Volunteers Saying?', *e-Volunteerism*, January/March 2003, www.e-volunteerism.com.

Cravens, Jayne, *Using Instant Messaging to Work with Volunteers: Benefits and Suggestions*, 2002 www.unites.org/Html/Resource/im/im0.htm

Culp, K and V Schwartz, 'Motivating Adult Volunteer 4-H Leaders', *Journal of Extension*, Vol. 37(1) 1999, www.joe.org/joe/1999february/rb5.html.

Culp, Ken and Vicki Schwartz, 'Recognizing Adult 4-H Volunteers', *Journal of Extension*, April 1998.

Culp, Ken, 'Identifying Continuing and Non-Continuing Adult 4-H Volunteers: How Have They Evolved Over Time?', *Journal of Agricultural Education*, Vol. 37(4) 1996.

Curtis, Allan, 'Landcare: Approaching the Limits of Voluntary Action', *Australian Journal of Environmental Management*, Vol. 7(1) 2000, www.regional.org. au/au/jc/j/2.htm.

Curtis, Allan, Marike van Nouhuys and Charles Sturt, 'Landcare Participation in Australia: The Volunteer Perspective', *Sustainable Development*, Vol. 7(2) 1999.

Cuskelly, G and A Boag, 'Organizational Commitment as a Predictor of Committee Member Turnover amongst Volunteer Sport Administrators: Results of a Time-Lagged Study', *Sport Management Review*, 2001.

Cuskelly, Graham, 'The Influence of Committee Functioning on the Organizational Commitment of Volunteer Administrators in Sports', *Journal of Sport Behavior*, December 1995.

Cuskelly, G, N McIntyre and A Boag, 'A Longitudinal Study of the Development of Organizational Commitment amongst Volunteer Sport Administrators', *Journal of Sport Behavior*, Vol. 18 1995.

Cyr, Carolyn and Peter Dowrick, 'Burnout in Crisisline Volunteers', *Administration and Policy in Mental Health*, May 1991.

Dailey, Robert, 'Understanding Organizational Commitment for Volunteers: Empirical and Managerial Implications', *Journal of Voluntary Action Research*, January/March 1986.

Daly, J, *Volunteers in South Australian Sport: A Study*, Canberra: Australian Sports Commission, 1991.

Danson, Mike, *Review of Research and Evidence on Volunteering*, Stirling: Volunteer Development Scotland, 2003.

Davis, MH, JA Hall and M Meyer, 'The First Year: Influences on the Satisfaction, Involvement and Persistence of New Community Volunteers', *Personality and Social Psychology Bulletin*, February 2003.

Davis Smith, Justin and Pat Gay, *Active Ageing in Active Communities: Volunteering and the Transition to Retirement*, York: Joseph Rowntree Foundation, 2005.

Dekimpe, MG and Z Degraeve, 'The Attrition of Volunteers', *European Journal of Operational Research*, April 1997.

DeMarco, John, 'Environmental Scan: Public Opinion and Communications Issues Regarding Volunteering and the Voluntary Sector', *Volunteer Action*, April 1998, www.lin.ca/resource/html/comenap2.htm

Disney, Diane, Sarah Jane Rehnborg, Laura Roberts, Julie Washburn and Vanda Williamson, 'Should Volunteers be Fired?', *Voluntary Action Leadership*, fall 1979.

Dorsch, Kim, Harold Reimer, Valerie Sluth, David Paskevich and Packianathan Chelladurai, *What Determines a Volunteer's Effort?* Toronto: Canadian Centre for Philanthropy, 2002.

Ellis, Susan, 'Barriers to Volunteering: Hidden Messages in Your Recruitment', *Nonprofit Times*, January 2002.

Ellis, Susan and Steve McCurley, 'Thinking the Unthinkable: Are We Using the Wrong Model for Volunteer Work?', *e-Volunteerism*, Vol. 3(3) 2003.

Elliston, Sarah, 'Integrity – the Guidepost to Volunteer Relationships', *e-Volunteerism*, October/December 2002, www.e-volunteerism.com.

Elstad, B, 'Continuance, Commitment and Reason to Quit: A Study of Volunteers at a Jazz Festival', *Event Management*, Vol. 8(2) 2003.

Environics Research Group, *Survey of Volunteer Managers*, Toronto: Canadian Centre for Philanthropy, 2003.

Erb, Joann, The Relationship between Perceived Self-Efficacy and Retention of New Hospice Volunteers, 2002, http://stti.confex.com/stti/sos13/techprogram/paper_11364.htm.

Esmond, Judy and Patrick Dunlop, *Developing the Volunteer Motivation Inventory to Assess the Underlying Motivational Drives of Volunteers in Western Australia*, East Perth: CLAN WA, 2004.

Fahey, Christine and Judi Walker, 'Asking Volunteers: The Development of Strategies to Improve Recruitment, Retention, Training and Support of Volunteer Ambulance Officers', Hobart: University Department of Public Health, University of Tasmania 2001.

Fahey, Christine, Judi Walker and Grant Lennox, 'Flexible, Focused Training Keeps Volunteer Ambulance Officers', *Journal of Emergency Primary Health Care*, Vol. 1(1-2) 2003.

Farmer, Steven and Donald Fedor, 'Changing the Focus on Volunteering: An Investigation of Volunteers' Multiple Contributions to a Charitable Organization', *Journal of Management*, March 2001.

Farmer, Steven and Donald Fedor, 'Volunteer Withdrawal and Participation', *Nonprofit Management and Leadership*, Vol. 9(4) 2003.

Feeney, Barbara, *Volunteering in Wellington*, Wellington, NZ: Wellington City Council, 2001, www.volunteerwellington.org.nz/iyvwccrep.htm.

FEMA, *Emergency Medical Services Recruitment and Retention Manual*, New York: United States Fire Administration, Federal Emergency Management Agency, 1995.

Field, D and I Johnson, 'Satisfaction and Change: A Survey of Volunteers in a Hospice Organisation', *Social Science Medicine*, June 1993.

Finkelstein, Marcia and Susan McIntyre, 'A Social Psychological Perspective on Recruitment and Retention of Hospice Volunteers', *Journal of Volunteer Administration*, Vol. 23(1), 2005.

Finn Paradis, L and W Usui, 'Volunteer Stress and Burnout: Issues for Administrators', *Hospice Journal*, Vol. 3(2/3) 1987.

Fischer, Lucy Rose and Kay Schaffer, *Older Volunteers: A Guide to Research and Practice*, Newbury Park: Sage Publications, 1993.

Fisher, Robert and David Ackerman, 'The Effects of Recognition and Group Need on Volunteerism: A Social Norm Perspective', *Journal of Consumer Research*, December 1998.

Fraser, Brenda and Ben Gottlieb, *Volunteers in Service to Long-Term Care Agencies: A Precious Resource under Pressure*, Guelph: Waterloo Region-Wellington-Dufferin District Health Council, 2001.

Frey, Bruno and Lorenz Goette, *Does Pay Motivate Volunteers?*, Zurich: Institute for Empirical Research in Economics, University of Zurich, 1999.

Fritz, S, J Barbato, David Marx, Arlen Etling and Shawn Burrow, 'Motivation and recognition preferences of 4-H volunteers', *Journal of Agricultural Education*, Vol. 41(3) pp. 40-49 2000.

Fritz, Susan, Deanna Karmazin, John Barbuto and Shawn Burrow, 'Urban and Rural 4-H Volunteer Leaders' Preferred Forms of Recognition and Motivation', *Journal of Extension*, June 2003.

Fryar, Andy, *Exploring the Social Side of Volunteer Involvement*, OzVPM, 2004, www.ozvpm.com.

Fuertes, Francisco and Maria Luisa Vecina Jimenez, *Motivation and Burnout in Volunteerism*, 2000, www.psychologyinspain.com/content/full/2000/7.htm.

Furano, Kathryn, Phoebe A Roaf, Melanie B Styles and Y Alvia, *Branch Big Brothers/Big Sisters: A Study of Program Practices*, Philadelphia: Public/Private Ventures, 1993.

Gabard, DL, 'Volunteer Burnout and Dropout: Issues in AIDS Service Organizations', *Journal of the Health and Human Services Administration*, winter 1997.

Galley, G and J Clifton, 'The Motivational and Demographic Characteristics of Research Ecotourists: Operation Wallacea Volunteers in Southeast Sulawesi, Indonesia',' *Journal of Ecotourism*, Vol. 3(1), 2004.

Gaskin, Katherine, *A Choice Blend: What Volunteers Want from Organisations and Management*, London: Institute for Volunteering Research, 2003.

George H Gallup International Institute, *Survey on Volunteering for Serious Social Problems*, Princeton: Gallup International Institute, 1995.

Gidron, B, 'Predictors of Retention and Turnover among Service Volunteer Workers', *Journal of Social Science Research*, fall 1984.

Ginsburg, Scott, 'Beyond the Mundane: Using Nametags to Build Community in Volunteer Groups,' *e-Volunteerism*, July/October 2004, www.e-volunteerism. com.

Glass, JC and JL Hastings, 'Stress and Burnout: Concerns for the Hospice Volunteer', *Educational Gerontology*, Vol. 18(7) pp. 717-31, 1992.

Glasser, William, *Control Theory*, New York: Harper Collins, 1985.

Goddin, Geoff, 'Whose Heritage Railway is It? A Study of Volunteer Motivation', *Japan Railway and Transport Review*, September 2002.

Gooch, Margaret, 'A Sense of Place: Ecological Identity as a Driver for Catchment Volunteering', *Australian Journal on Volunteering*, Vol. 8(2) pp. 193-208, 2003 www.coastal.crc.org.au/pdf/ RRR03/RRR03_Gooch_Senseof place.pdf.

Gora, Jo Ann and Gloria Nemerowicz, 'Volunteers: Initial and Sustaining Motivations in Service to the Community', *Research in the Sociology of Health Care*, Vol. 9, 1991.

Goss, Kristin, 'Volunteering and the Long Civic Generation', *Nonprofit and Voluntary Sector Quarterly*, December 1999.

GoVolunteer, GoVolunteer User Research Report, Melbourne: Volunteering Australia, 2004, www.go volunteer.com.au

Graff, Linda, *By Definition: Policies for Volunteer Programs*, Etobicoke: Volunteer Ontario, 1993.

Graff, Linda, 'Policies for Volunteer Programs', in Tracy Connors, ed., *The Volunteer Management Handbook*, New York: John Wiley and Sons, 1995.

Greenberg, Liane, *Giving and Volunteering in Alberta*, Toronto: Canadian Centre for Philanthropy, 1997.

Griffiths, Megan, *A Study of the Motivations and Characteristics of Meals on Wheels Volunteers*, 2003, www.nswmealsonwheels.org.au/pdf/motivational.pdf.

Grossman, Jean and Kathryn Furano, *Making the Most of Volunteers*, Philadelphia: Public/Private Ventures, 2002.

Grossman, Jean and Jean Rhodes, 'The Test of Time: Predictors and Effects of Duration in Youth Mentoring Relationships', *American Journal of Community Psychology*, April 2002.

Grube, J and J Piliavin, 'Role Identity, Organizational Experiences and Volunteer Performance', *Personality and Social Psychology Bulletin*, September 2000.

Guinan, JJ, LW McCallum, L Painter, J Dykes and J Gold, 'Stressors and Rewards of being an AIDS Emotional-Support Volunteer: A Scale for Use by Care-Givers for People with AIDS', *AIDS Care*, Vol. 3(2) 1991.

Guseh, James and Rebecca Winders, 'A Profile of Volunteerism in North Carolina', *Journal of Volunteer Administration*, Vol. 20(4) 2002.

Hager, Mark and Jeffrey Brudney, *Volunteer Management Practices and Retention of Volunteers*, Washington: Urban Institute, 2004.

Hall, Michael, A-J McKechnie, Katie Davidman and Fleur Leslie, *An Environmental Scan on Volunteering and Improving Volunteering*, Toronto: Canadian Centre for Philanthropy, 2001.

Hall, Michael, Larry McKeown and Karen Roberts, *Caring Canadians, Involved Canadians: Highlights of the 2000 National Survey of Giving, Volunteering and Participating*, Toronto: Canadian Centre for Philanthropy, 2001.

Hanawi, Nancy, 'An Interactive Model for Volunteerism', Working Paper #14, Institute for Nonprofit Organization Management, University of San Francisco, 1990.

'Hands for Nature, Summary Report on Community Greening', in *Volunteerism 2002*, Ontario: Hands for Nature, 2002.

Handy, Femida and Narasimhan Srinivasan, *Costs and Contributions of Professional Volunteer Management: Lessons from Ontario Hospitals*, Toronto: Canadian Centre for Philanthropy, 2003.

Handy, Femida, Robert Mound, Lisa-Marie Vaccaro and Karin Prochazka, *Promising Practices for Volunteer Administration in Hospitals*, Toronto: Canadian Centre for Philanthropy, 2004.

Hashim, Mohamed Aris, 'Recruiting and Retaining Volunteers', *Hemophilia Organization Development*, No. 3, July 2003.

Hawthorne, Nan, 'Customer Service for Volunteer Programs', *Volunteer Management Review*, 10 April 2002, http://charitychannel.com/article_171.shtml.

Hawthorne, Nan, 'Preventing Volunteer Burnout', *Volunteer Management Review*, 15 May 2002, http://charitychannel.com/article_166.shtml.

Heritage Link, *Volunteers and the Historic Environment*, London: Heritage Link, 2003, www.heritagelink.org.uk/publications.asp

Heidrich, Kathryn, *Working with Volunteers in Employee Services and Recreation Programs*, Champaign: Sagamore Publishing, 1990.

Heyworth, Peter and Andy Fryar, *In from the CALD*, OzVPM, 2004, www.ozvpm.com.

Hobbs, Beverly, *Recruiting and Supporting Latino Volunteers*, Corvallis, OR: Pacific Northwest Extension, 2000.

Hobson, CJ, Kathryn Heler and Constance Milbourne, 'Is Your Campaign Really Volunteer-Friendly?', *Campaigns & Elections*, September 2002.

Hobson, CJ, A Rominger, K Malec, CL Hobson, and K Evans, 'Volunteer Friendliness of Nonprofit Agencies: Definition, Conceptual Model, and Applications', *Journal of Nonprofit and Public Sector Marketing*, Vol. 44(4), pp. 27-41, 1996.

Hobson, Charles and Kathryn Malec, 'Initial Telephone Contact of Prospective Volunteers with Nonprofits: An Operational Definition of Quality and Norms for 500 Agencies', *Journal of Volunteer Administration*, summer/fall 1999.

Holden, Daphne, 'On Equal Ground: Sustaining Virtue among Volunteers in a Homeless Shelter', *Journal of Contemporary Ethnography*, July 1997.

Hollway, S, 'Vital Volunteers', *Australian Leisure Management*, Vol. 30, December/January 2001/02.

Holmes, Kirsten, *Volunteer Motivation: A Theoretical and Empirical Review*, Discussion Paper No. 2003.02, University of Sheffield Management School, 2003.

Howell, Albert, *Why do Volunteers Burnout and Dropout?* Calgary: Research Unit for Public Policy Studies, University of Calgary, 1986.

Hunot, Vivian and Alan Rosenbach, 'Factors Influencing the Attitudes and Commitment of Volunteer Alcohol Counsellors', *British Journal of Guidance and Counselling*, August 1998.

Hustinx, Lesley, 'Beyond the Tyranny of the New? An Explanatory Model of Styles of Flemish Red Cross Volunteering', paper presented at ECPR Joint Sessions of Workshops, Uppsala, April 13-18 2004.

Ilsley, Paul, *Enhancing the Volunteer Experience*, San Francisco: Jossey-Bass, 1990.

Independent Sector, *Giving and Volunteering in the United States*, 2001 Washington: Independent Sector, 2000.

Institute for Volunteering Research, *1997 National Survey of Volunteering in the UK*, 1997 www.ivr.org.uk.nationalsurvey.htm.

Institute for Volunteering Research, 'Age Discrimination and Volunteering', *Research Bulletin*, 1999, www.ivr.org.uk/age.htm.

Institute for Volunteering Research, *Issues in Volunteer Management: A Report of a Survey*, London: IVR 1998, www.ivr.org.uk/issues.htm.

Institute for Volunteering Research, *Volunteering for All? Exploring the Link between Volunteering and Social Exclusion*, London: IVR 2003, www.ivr.org.uk/social exclusion/index.htm

International Centre for Research and Consultancy for the Tourism and Hospitality Industries, *Sports Development Impact of the Commonwealth Games: Study of Volunteers*, Manchester: Manchester Metropolitan University, 2003.

Jamison, Irma Browne, 'Turnover and Retention among Volunteers in Human Service Agencies', *Review of Public Personnel Administration*, June 2003.

JC Penny Company, 'A National Profile – Volunteering', Washington: VOLUNTEER – The National Center, 1987.

Johnson, Monica, Kristie Foley and Glen Elder, 'Women's Community Service, 1940-1960: Insights from a Cohort of Gifted American Women', *Sociological Quarterly*, Vol. 45(1), 2004.

Johnston, Margaret E, G David Twynam and Jocelyn M Farrell, 'Motivation and Satisfaction of Event Volunteers for a Major Youth Organization', *Leisure/Loisir*, Vol. 24(1-2) pp. 161-77 1999-2000.

Kearney, MM and SH Carpenter, 'Motivation and Commitment of Hospice Volunteers', *American Journal of Hospice Care*, fall 1984.

Keaveney, Susan, Marilyn Saltzman and Nancy Sullivan, 'Volunteers as Customers: A Service Quality Perspective', *Journal of Volunteer Administration*, fall 1991.

Keyton, Joanne, Gerald Wilson and Cheryl Geiger, 'Improving Volunteer Commitment to Organizations', *Journal of Volunteer Administration*, summer 1990.

Knapp, Martin, *Who Volunteers and Why? Key Factors Which Determine Volunteering*, London: Volunteer Centre UK, 1995.

Kuyper, Joan, *Volunteer Program Administration: A Handbook for Museums and Other Cultural Institutions*, New York: American Council for the Arts, 1993.

Lafer, B, 'Predicting Performance and Persistence in Hospice Volunteers', *Psychological Reports*, October 1989.

Lake Snell Perry & Associates, *Short-Term Impacts, Long-Term Opportunities: The Political and Civic Engagement of Young Adults in America*, Washington: Center for Information and Research in Civic Learning and Engagement, 2002.

Lake, Vern, '101 Ways to Give Recognition to Volunteers', *Voluntary Action Leadership*, winter 1977.

Lammers, John, 'Attitudes, Motives, and Demographic Predictors of Volunteer Commitment and Service Duration', *Journal of Social Service Research*, Vol. 14(3/4) 1991.

Lasby, David, *The Volunteer Spirit in Canada: Motivations and Barriers*, Toronto: Canadian Centre for Philanthropy, 2004.

Latting, Jean Kantambu, 'Motivational Differences between Black and White Volunteers', *Nonprofit and Voluntary Sector Quarterly*, summer 1990.

Lee, Jarene and Julie Catagnus, *Supervising Volunteers*, Philadelphia: Energize, 1999.

LeRoy, Sylvia and Jason Clemens, *2003 Non-Profit Performance Report: An Analysis of Management, Staff, Volunteers, and Board Effectiveness in the Non-Profit Sector,* Vancouver: Fraser Institute, 2003.

Leisure Industries Research Centre, *Sports Volunteering in England 2002,* London: Sport England, 2003.

Leonard, Rosemary and Alisa Burns, 'Personal Agency and Public Recognition in Women's Volunteering: Does the Organisation Make a Difference?', *Australian Journal on Volunteering,* Vol. 8(2), 2003.

Liao-Troth, Matthew, 'Job Attitudes of Paid and Unpaid Workers: Are Volunteers Really that Different?', *Nonprofit Management and Leadership,* Vol. 11(4) 2001.

Li-Kook, Joueon, *Reconsidering the Nature of Episodic Volunteering: A Case Study of Event Volunteers,* 2002, www.diversitylab.uiuc.edu/abstract_ yi.html.

Lindhorst, Taryn and Ronald Mancoske, 'Structuring Support for Volunteer Commitment: An AIDS Services Program Study', *Journal of Sociology and Social Welfare,* March 1993.

Litwin, Howard and Abraham Monk, 'Volunteer Ombudsman Burnout in Long Term Care Services: Some Causes and Solutions', *Administration in Social Work,* spring 1984.

Lopez, Mark Hugo, *Volunteering among Young People,* Washington DC: Center for Information and Research on Civic Learning & Engagement, 2004.

Lucas, T and N Williams, 'Motivation as a Function of Volunteer Retention', *Australian Journal on Volunteering,* Vol. 5(1) 2000.

Luffman, Jacqueline and Mary Cromie, 'The Culture of Volunteering and Donating: Helping Culture Organizations between 1997 and 2000', *Focus on Culture,* Vol. 14(2), June 2003.

Lynch, Richard, 'Volunteer Retention and Feelings of Connection', *e-Volunteerism,* July/September 2002.

Lysakowski, Linda, 'What's in It for Me?', in Rebecca Hunter, ed., *Exploring the Relationship between Volunteers and Fundraisers, New Directions in Philanthropic Fundraising,* Bloomington, IN: Center on Philanthropy, Indiana University, Spring 2003.

Macduff, Nancy, 'Episodic Volunteering', in Tracy Connors, ed., *The Volunteer Management Handbook,* New York: John Wiley and Sons, 1995.

Macduff, Nancy, 'Retention: the Pluses and Minuses of Volunteers', *Voluntary Action Leadership,* winter 1992.

Macduff, Nancy, 'Societal Changes and the Rise of the Episodic Volunteer', in Jeffrey Brudney, ed., *Emerging Areas of Volunteering*, ARNOVA Occasional Paper Series, Vol. 1(2), 2005.

Maslanka, H, 'Burnout, Social Support and AIDS Volunteers', *AIDS Care*, April 1996.

McClintock, Norah, *Understanding Canadian Volunteers: Using the National Survey of Giving, Volunteering and Participating to Build Your Volunteer Program*, Toronto: Canadian Centre for Philanthropy, 2004.

McComb, Mary, 'Becoming a Travelers Aid Volunteer: Communication in Socialization and Training', *Communication Studies*, Vol. 46(3) 1995.

McCudden, Jackie, 'What Makes a Committed Volunteer? Research into the Factors affecting the Retention of Volunteers in Home-Start', *Voluntary Action*, spring 2000.

McCune, Bonnie and Charlezine Nelson, *Recruiting and Managing Volunteers in Libraries*, New York: Neal-Schuman Publishers, 1995.

McCurley, Steve, 'Analyzing Customer Service in Volunteer Programs', *Grapevine*, May/June 2001.

McCurley, Steve, 'Answering the Unasked Questions of Volunteers', *Grapevine*, January/February 2005.

McCurley, Steve, 'Case Study: The Changing World of Hospital Volunteering', in Sue Vineyard and Steve McCurley, *Best Practices for Volunteer Programs*, Downers Grove: Heritage Arts, 2001.

McCurley, Steve, 'Creating a Volunteer-Friendly Organization', *Grapevine*, September/October 2004.

McCurley, Steve, 'Fishing for Volunteers: Using Short-Term Projects to Catch Long-Term Volunteers', *Grapevine*, May/June 1998.

McCurley, Steve, 'Recruiting and Retaining Volunteers', in *The Jossey-Bass Handbook of Nonprofit Leadership and Management*, Robert Herman, ed, San Francisco: Jossey Bass, 2004.

McCurley, Steve, 'The Sleeping Giant: Alternative Futures for Hospital Volunteering', *Volunteer Leader*, spring 1999.

McCurley, Steve and Rick Lynch, *Volunteer Management*, Downers Grove: Heritage Arts, 1996.

McCurley, Steve and Sue Vineyard, *Handling Problem Volunteers*, Downers Grove: Heritage Arts, 1998.

McMurray, Peter, *Early Match Closures – A Qualitative Study*, Big Brothers of Ontario, 1993, www.mentoringcanada.ca/Doclibrary/docdisplay.asp?doc=1303.

McSweeney, Phil and Don Alexander, *Managing Volunteers Effectively*, Hampshire: Arena Ashgate Publishing Limited, 1996.

Meikle, Tunde, 'Burnout in the Fire Service: The Work-Life Imbalance of Volunteer Firefighters', *Australian Journal on Volunteering*, Vol. 6(2) 2001.

Merrell, J, 'Ambiguity: Exploring the Complexity of Roles and Boundaries when Working with Volunteers in Well Woman Clinics', *Social Science & Medicine*, July 2000.

Merrell, J, 'You Don't Do It for Nothing: Women's Experiences of Volunteering in Two Community Well Woman Clinics', *Health and Social Care in the Community*, January 2000.

Merrill, Mary, *Firing a Volunteer*, July 2002 www.merrillassociates.net

Merrill, Mary, *Nurturing Spirit through Recognition*, 2002 www.merrill associates.net

Michael, Bernard, ed., *Volunteers in Public Schools*, Washington: National Academy Press, 1990.

Mihalicz, Dwight and Swee Goh, 'The Relationship between Volunteer Motivations and Behavior in Non-Profit Organizations', *Journal of Volunteer Administration*, fall 1996.

Miller, Kimberly, Stuart Schleien, Cecilia Rider and Crystal Hall, 'Inclusive Volunteering: Benefits to Participants and Community', *Therapeutic Recreation Journal*, July 2002.

Miller, L, 'Understanding the Motivation of Volunteers: An Examination of Personality Differences and Characteristics of Volunteers' Paid Employment', *Journal of Voluntary Action Research*, 1985.

Miller, LE, GN Powell and J Seltzer, 'Determinants of Turnover among Volunteers', *Human Relations*, Vol. 9, 1990.

Monga, M and G Treuren, 'Employment Relations without Paid Work: An Exploration into the HRM and Motivations of Special Event Volunteers', paper presented at the International Relations Association 2001 Annual Conference, Singapore, http://business.unisa.edu.au/cae/projects/current/seo/MongaTreuren.pdf.

Morrow-Howell, N and A Mui, 'Elderly Volunteers: Reasons for Initiating and Terminating Service', *Journal of Gerontological Social Work*, 1987.

Musgrove, Doug, 'Don't Leave Me This Way', *Volunteering*, November 2001.

Mutchler, J, J Burr and F Caro, 'Volunteer Work and Burnout in Later Life', *Gerontologist*, 15 October 2001.

Nassar-McMilllan, S and R Lambert, 'The Relationship between Volunteers' Work Behaviors and Background and Preparation Variables', *Journal of Adult Development*, April 2003.

Nathanson, Ilene and Elizabeth Eggleton, 'Motivation versus Program Effect on Length of Service: A Study of Four Cohorts of Ombudservice Volunteers', *Journal of Gerontological Social Work*, January 1993.

National Committee on Volunteering, *Tipping the Balance: Report of the National Committee on Volunteering*, Dublin: National Committee on Volunteering, 2002.

National Health and Medical Research Council, *Working with Volunteers and Managing Volunteers in Health Care Settings*, Canberra: NHMRC, 2003.

National Volunteer and Philanthropy Centre, *2002 Survey on Volunteerism in Singapore*, NVPC: Singapore, www.nvc.org.sg/resources/Survey2002/highlights. html#2002.

Nelson, H Wayne, Clara Pratt, Charles Carpenter and Kathy Walter, 'Factors Affecting Volunteer Long-Term Care Ombudsman Organizational Commitment and Burnout', *Nonprofit and Voluntary Sector Quarterly*, fall 1995.

Nelson, H Wayne, Ellen Netting, Kevin Borders and Ruth Huber, 'Volunteer Attrition: Lessons Learned from Oregon's Long-Term Care Ombudsman Program', *Journal of Volunteer Administration*, Vol. 22(2), 2004a.

Nelson, H Wayne, Karen Hooker, Kimberly DeHart, John Edwards and Kevin Lanning, 'Factors Important to Success in the Volunteer Long-Term Care Ombudsman Role', *The Gerontologist*, February 2004b.

Nesbitt, WH, MW Ross, RH Sunderland, and E Shelp, 'Prediction of grief and HIV/AIDS-related burnout in volunteers'. *AIDS Care*, Vol. 8, pp. 137-43, 1996.

Netting, E, R Huber, K Borders, JR Kautz and HW Nelson, 'Volunteer and Paid Ombudsmen Investigating Complaints in Six States: A Natural Triaging', *Nonprofit and Voluntary Sector Quarterly*, Vol. 29(3) 2000.

Newton, Lucy, 'A Study of Attitudes and Perceptions of Volunteers in Nonprofit Organizations', *Journal of Volunteer Administration*, winter 1995.

Nichols, Geoff, *The Tension between Professionalisation and Volunteerism in English National Governing Bodies of Sport*, Discussion Paper Series No. 2003.12, Leisure Management Division, Sheffield University Management School, 2003.

Nichols, Geoff and Lindsay King, 'The Changing Motivations and Frustrations Facing Volunteers in Youth Groups: A Study of the Guide Association of the United Kingdom', *Journal of Applied Recreation Research*, Vol. 23(3) 1999.

Noble, Joy, Louise Rogers and Andy Fryar, 'Volunteer Management: An Essential Guide', *Volunteering SA*, 2003.

Northstar Research Partners, *Big Brothers and Sisters of Canada: A Qualitative Report*, Toronto: Northstar Research Partners, 1999.

Oesterle, Sabrina, Monica Johnson and Jeylan Mortimer, 'Volunteerism during the Transition to Adulthood', *Social Forces*, Vol. 83(2) 2004.

Ogilvie, Robert, *Voluntarism, Community Life and the American Ethic*, Bloomington, IN: Indiana University Press, 2004.

Okun, Morris, 'The Relation between Motives for Organizational Volunteering and Frequency of Volunteering', *Journal of Applied Gerontology*, Vol. 13(2) 1994.

Omoto, Allen and Mark Snyder, 'Sustained Helping without Obligation: Motivation, Longevity of Service and Perceived Attitude Change among AIDS Volunteers', *Journal of Personality and Social Psychology*, April 1995.

Omoto, Allen, Mark Snyder and Steven Martino, 'Volunteerism and the Life Course: Investigating Age-Related Agendas for Action', *Basic and Applied Social Psychology*, Vol. 22(3) 2000.

Ontario Ministry of Tourism and Recreation, *Ontario Volunteers in Sport, Fitness and Recreation*, Toronto: Ministry of Tourism and Recreation, 1990, www.lin.ca/resource/html/volu.htm.

O'Rourke, Molly, 'How the Internet Changed Volunteering: Findings from a VolunteerMatch User Study', *Journal of Volunteer Administration*, Vol. 22(3) 2004.

Osborne, LJ, 'Re-engaging Service Personnel as Volunteers after Deployment', *Extension Extra*, April 2004, http://sdces.sdstate.edu/ces_website/hit_counter.cfm?item=ExEx15012&id=1006

Pankaj, Vibha, *Ethnic Minority Volunteering in Scotland: A Perspective of Mainstream Organisations*, Stirling: Volunteer Development Scotland, 2002.

Paradis, Lenora and Wayne Usui, 'Hospice Volunteers: The Impact of Personality Characteristics on Retention and Job Performance', *The Hospice Journal*, spring, 1987.

Peach, E Brian and Kenneth Murrell, 'Reward and Recognition Systems for Volunteers', in Tracy Connors, ed., *The Volunteer Management Handbook*, New York: John Wiley and Sons, 1995.

Pearce, Jone, 'Job Attitude and Motivation Differences between Volunteers and Employees from Comparable Organizations', *Journal of Applied Psychology*, Vol. 4 1983.

Pearce, Jone, 'Managing Volunteers: The Role of Ambiguity in Volunteer Motivation', in RD Herman, *Politics, Public Policy and the Voluntary Sector*, Kansas City: University of Missouri-Kansas City, 1987.

Pearce, Jone, *Volunteers – The Organizational Behaviour of Unpaid Workers*, London: Routledge, 1993.

Penner, Louise, 'Dispositional and Organizational Issues on Sustained Volunteerism: An Interactionist Perspective', *Journal of Social Issues*, fall 2002.

Perkins, Kenneth, 'Volunteer Fire and Rescue Corporations: Structure, Process and Survival', *Nonprofit and Voluntary Sector Quarterly*, Vol. 19(4) 1990.

Persson, Diane, 'Volunteer Ombudsmen in the Nursing Home: Obstacles to Retention', *Journal of Aging Studies*, May 2004.

Peter D Hart Research Associates, *VolunteerMatch Research Findings*, Washington, DC: Peter D Hart Research Associates, 2004.

Phibbs, Peter, *Rural and Regional Volunteering Support*, Sydney: Premier's Department, New South Wales, 2003, www.communitybuilders.nsw.gov.au/builder/volunteering/vol_supp.html

Phillips, Susan, Brian Little and Laura Goodine, *Caregiving Volunteers: A Coming Crisis?* Toronto: Canadian Centre for Philanthropy, 2002.

Phillips, Susan, Brian Little and Laura Goodine, *Recruiting, Retaining and Rewarding Volunteers: What Volunteers Have to Say*, Toronto: Canadian Centre for Philanthropy, 2002.

Phillips, William and Joan Bradshaw, 'Florida Master Gardener Mentor Program: A Case Study', *Journal of Extension*, August 1999, www.joe.org.

Pierucci, J and R Noel, 'Duration of Participation of Correctional Volunteers as a Function of Personal and Situational Variables', *Journal of Community Psychology*, 1980.

Points of Light Foundation, *Assessing the Volunteer Paradigm: A Report on Volunteerism among the Nation's Health Agencies*, Washington: Points of Light Foundation, 1996.

Princeton Survey Research Associates, *The Do Something Inc. Young People's Community Involvement Survey*, Princeton: PSRA, 1998.

Propst, Dennis and Stephen Bentley, *Trends in Citizen Participation in Outdoor Recreation and Resource Management: Manager vs. Citizen Perspectives*, 2000, www.prr.msu.edu/trends2000/pdf/propst_partic.pdf.

Public/Private Ventures, *Supporting Mentors*, Philadelphia, PA: National Mentoring Center, Northwest Regional Educational Library, 2001.

Qureshi, Hazel, Bleddyn Davies and David Challis, 'Motivations and Rewards of Volunteers and Informal Care Givers', *Journal of Voluntary Action Research*, Vol. 8(1/2) 1979.

Raskoff, Sally and Richard Sundeen, 'Community Service Programs in High Schools', *Law and Contemporary Problems*, autumn 1999.

Raskoff, Sally and Richard Sundeen, 'Cultural Diversity and High School Community Service', *Nonprofit and Voluntary Sector Quarterly*, December 2001.

Reich, WA, 'Identity Structure, Narrative Accounts and Commitment to a Volunteer Role', *Journal of Psychology*, July 2000.

Reilly, Christine, *A Way of Life: Black and Minority Ethnic Diverse Communities as Volunteers*, Stirling: Volunteer Development Scotland, 2004.

Riemer, Harold, Kim Dorsch, Larena Hoeber, David Paskevich and Pachianathan Chelladurai, *Motivations for Volunteering with Youth-Oriented Programs*, Toronto: Canadian Centre for Philanthropy, 2004.

Roaf, Phoebe, Joseph Tierney and Danista Hunte, *Big Brother/Big Sisters: A Study of Volunteer Recruitment and Screening*, (Philadelphia: Public/Private Ventures) 1994.

Rog, Evelina, Mark Pancer and Mark Baetz, 'Corporate Volunteer Programs: Maximizing Employee Motivation and Minimizing Barriers to Program Participation', Toronto: Canadian Centre for Philanthropy, 2003.

Rogers, Bill, 'Developing a Successful Mentoring Program for Volunteer Training', *Journal of Extension*, October 1997, www.joe.org.

Ross, MW, SA Greenfield and L Bennett, 'Predictors of Dropout and Burnout in AIDS Volunteers: A Longitudinal Study', *AIDS Care*, December 1999.

Rubin, A and L Thorelli, 'Egoistic Motives and Longevity of Participation by Social Service Volunteers', *Journal of Applied Behavioral Sciences*, Vol. 20(3), pp. 223-35 1984.

Russell Commission, *A National Framework for Youth Action and Engagement*, Report of the Russell Commission, Norwich, UK: HMSO, 2005, www.russell commission.org.

Ryan, RL, R Kaplan and RE Grese, 'Predicting Volunteer Commitment in Environmental Stewardship Programmes', *Journal of Environmental Planning and Management*, Vol. 44(5) 2001.

Sadler, Larry and Frank Marty, 'Socialization of Hospice Volunteers: Members of the Family', *Hospice Journal*, Vol. 13(3) 1998.

Safrit, Dale, *Volunteerism among Gen Xers: A Glimpse at the Motivations and Interests of 4-H's Future Volunteers*, Washington, DC: US Department of Agriculture, www.reeusda.gov/f4hn/v2k/Volunteerism_Among_Generation_Xers.htm, 2001.

Scheier, Ivan, 'Improving Volunteer Motivation through Job Design', in Larry Moore, ed., *Motivating Volunteers: How the Rewards of Unpaid Work can Meet People's Needs*, Vancouver: Volunteer Centre, 1985.

Scott, Jean Pearson and Jackie Caldwell, 'Needs and Program Strengths: Perceptions of Hospice Volunteers', *Hospice Journal*, Vol. 11(1) 1996.

Segal, L, *Four Essays on the Supply of Volunteer Labor and Econometrics*, unpublished doctoral dissertation, Chicago: Northwestern University, 1993.

Selbee, Kevin and Paul Reed, 'Patterns of Volunteering over the Life Cycle', *Canadian Social Trends*, summer 2001.

Selig, Susan and Danny Borton, 'Keeping Volunteers in EMS', *Voluntary Action Leadership*, fall 1989.

Simpson, Charles, 'A Fraternity of Danger: Volunteer Fire Companies and the Contradiction of Modernization', *American Journal of Economics and Sociology*, January 1996.

Slaughter, Lee and Robert Home, *Motivations of Long Term Volunteers: Human Services versus Events*, Brisbane: School of Tourism and Leisure Management, University of Queensland, 2004, http://hotel.unlv.edu/pdf/MotivationsofLT volunteers.pdf.

Smith, Karen, 'Literary Enthusiasts as Visitors and Volunteers', *International Journal of Tourism Research*, Vol. 5(2) 2003.

Smith, Keith and Nancy Bigler, 'Keeping 4-H Volunteer Leaders', *Journal of Extension*, summer 1985.

Smith, RP, 'Mental Health Status of World Trade Center Rescue and Recovery Workers and Volunteers', *MMWR Weekly*, 10 September 2004, www.cdc.gov/mmwr/preview/mmwrhtml/mm5335.htm.

Sport England, *Sports Volunteering in England in 2002: A Summary Report*, London: Sport England, 2003.

Starnes, Becky and Walter Wymer, 'Demographics, Personality Traits, Roles, Motivations and Attritions Rates of Hospice Volunteers', *Journal of Nonprofit and Public Sector Marketing*, Vol. 7(2) 1999.

Statistics Canada, *Cornerstones of Community: Highlights of the National Survey of Nonprofit and Voluntary Organizations, Small Business and Special Surveys Division*, Ottawa: Statistics Canada, 2004.

Steele, Sara, *Volunteers in Action: Summary of Phase II Conclusions and Implications*, Madison: Department of Continuing and Vocational Education, University of Wisconsin-Madison, 1986.

Stevens, ES, 'Toward Satisfaction and Retention of Senior Volunteers', *Journal of Gerontological Social Work*, Vol. 16(3/4) 1991.

Stevick, Richard and John Addleman, 'Effects of Short-term Volunteer Experiences on Self-perceptions and Prosocial Behavior', *Journal of Social Psychology*, October 1995.

Stewart, Eric and Rhona Weinstein, 'Volunteer Participation in Context: Motivation and Political Efficacy within Three AIDS Organizations', *Journal of Community Psychology*, December 1997.

Stewart, SH, TL Mitchell, KD Wright and P Loba, 'The Relations of PTSD Symptoms to Alcohol Use and Coping Drinking in Volunteers who Responded to the Swissair Flight 111 Airline Disaster', *Journal of Anxiety Disorder*, Vol. 18(1) 2004.

Stills, Michael Lee, 'Retiring with Dignity: Volunteer Emeritus Programs', *Volunteer Management Review*, 13 May 2003, http://charitychannel.com/article_5374.shtml.

Strategic Volunteering Advisory Group and Isabella Mori, *The Strategic Volunteering Report*, Vancouver: Strathcona Community Center, 2001, www.vcn.bc.ca/skillsco/svreport.htm.

Stukas, AA, J Haugen and P Meine, 'Understanding and Assessing the Motivations of Volunteers: A Functional Approach', *Journal of Personality and Social Psychology*, Vol. 74, pp. 1516-30 1998.

Stukas, A, M Snyder and EG Clary, 'The Effects of "Mandatory Volunteerism" on Intentions to Volunteer', *Psychological Science*, January 1999.

Taylor, Peter, et al, *Sports Volunteering in England 2002 – A Report for Sport England*, Sheffield: Leisure Industries Research Centre, 2003.

Taylor, Peter, 'Driving Up Participation: Sport and Volunteering', in Rowe, N, *Driving Up Participation: The Challenge for Sport*, London: Sport England, 2004.

Thinktank Research Consultancy, *Volunteerism in Sport*, Hong Kong: Sports Development Board, 1997.

Thompson, Alexander and Barbara Bono, 'Work without Wages: The Motivation for Volunteer Firefighters', *American Journal of Economics and Sociology*, autumn 1993.

Tillman, John, 'Sustainability of Heritage Railways: An Economic Approach', *Japan Railway and Transport Review*, September 2002.

Tillman, Marie, 'Motivating Volunteers at the National Aquarium in Baltimore', *Communique*, April 2003.

Toronto Community and Neighborhood Services, *Cracks in the Foundation: A Study of Toronto's Community-Based Human Service Sector*, Toronto: TCNS, 2004.

Tschirhart, Mary, Debra Mesch, James Perry, Theodore Miller and Geunjoo Lee, 'Stipended Volunteers: Their Goals, Experiences, Satisfaction and Likelihood of Future Service', *Nonprofit and Voluntary Sector Quarterly*, September 2001.

UK Sport, *An Evaluation of the Motivations and Expectations of Volunteers Prior to the XVII Commonwealth Games*, Manchester: UK Sport, 2002.

UMR Research, *Developing a Strategy to Nurture, Enhance and Expand the Volunteer Fire Brigade*, New Zealand Fire Service Commission Report #23, Aukland: UMR Research, 2001.

United Parcel Service Foundation, *Managing Volunteers*, Nashville: UPS, 1998.

Urban Institute, *Volunteer Management Capacity in America's Charities and Congregations: A Briefing Report*, Washington: Urban Institute, 2004.

Valeriote, T, 'Building Commitment for the Volunteer Program: A Replicable Model', *Journal of Volunteer Administration*, Vol. 17(2) 1999.

Vineyard, Sue, *Recognizing Volunteers and Paid Staff*, Darien, IL: Heritage Arts, 2001.

Volunteer Development Scotland, *Findings from the NFO System Three Scottish Opinion Survey*, Stirling: Volunteer Development Scotland, 2003.

Wandersman, A and J Alderman, 'Incentives, Costs and Barriers for Volunteers: A Staff Perspective on Volunteers in One State', *Review of Public Personnel Administration*, Vol. 13, 1993.

Wang, C and FD Ashbury, *Motivational and Retention Factors for Volunteering with the CCS*, Toronto: Centre for Behavioural Research and Program Evaluation, National Cancer Institute of Canada, 1997.

Watts, Ann and Patricia Edwards, 'Recruiting and Retaining Human Service Volunteers: An Empirical Analysis', *Journal of Voluntary Action Research*, July/September 1983.

Weston, Michael, Michael Fendley, Robyn Jewell, Mary Satchell and Chris Tzaro, 'Volunteers in Bird Conservation: Insights from the Australian Threatened Bird Network', *Ecological Management & Restoration*, Vol. 4(3), December 2003.

White, David and Mary Arnold, 'Why They Come, Why They Go, and Why They Stay: Factors Affecting Volunteerism in 4-H Programs', *Journal of Extension*, August 2003.

White, Geoffrey, 'Near Ground Zero: Compassion Fatigue in the Aftermath of September 11', *Traumatology*, December 2001.

Whitney, David and Michael Lindell, 'Member Commitment and Participation in Local Emergency Planning Committees', *Policy Studies Journal*, Vol. 28(3) 2000.

Wilson, Carla, Anne Hendricks and Rachel Smithies, 'Lady Bountiful and the Virtual Volunteers: The Changing Face of Social Service Volunteering', *Social Policy Journal of New Zealand*, December 2001.

Wilson, J and M Musick, 'Attachment to Volunteering', *Sociological Forum*, June 1999.

Wolfberg, DM, 'The Truth about Volunteer Incentives: The Pros and Cons of Administrating an EMS Volunteer Incentive Program', *Journal of Emergency Medical Service*, August 1998.

Wollebaek, Dag and Per Selle, 'Generations and Organizational Change', in Paul Dekker and Loek Halman, eds, *The Values of Volunteering: Cross-Cultural Perspectives*, New York: Kluwer Academic/Plenum Publishers, 2003.

Wu, Homer, *Exploring the Relationship between Motivation and Job Satisfaction of Volunteer Interpreters: A Case Study from Taiwan's National Park*, Taipei, Taiwan: National Park Society, Proceedings of IUCN/WCP-EA-4 Taipei Conference, March 2002.

Wymer, Walter, 'A Qualitative Analysis of Church Volunteerism: Motives for Service, Motives for Retention, and Perceived Benefits/Rewards from Volunteering', *Journal of Ministry Marketing and Management*, Vol. 5(1) 1999.

Yan, EC and CS Tang, 'The Role of Individual, Interpersonal and Organizational Factors in Mitigating Burnout among Elderly Chinese Volunteers', *International Journal of Geriatric Psychiatry*, September 2003.

Yi-Kook, Jouyen, *Reconsidering the Nature of Episodic Volunteering: A Case Study of Event Volunteers*, Diversity Research Laboratory, Department of Leisure Studies, University of Illinois at Urbana-Champaign, 2002, www.diversity lab.uiuc.edu/abstract_cclr2002_yi.html

Yufe, Ona, 'When Volunteers Grieve', *Journal of Volunteer Administration*, spring 1998.

Zappala, Gianni and Tracy Burrell, *The Giving of Time and Money: An Analysis of Donor Behavior among Volunteers*, Working Paper No. 7, Sydney: Research and Social Policy Team, The Smith Family, 2002, www.smithfamily.com.au.

Zappala Gianni and Tracy Burrell, *Why are Some Volunteers More Committed than Others? A Socio-Psychological Approach to Volunteer Commitment in Community Services*, Working Paper No. 5, Sydney: Research and Social Policy Team, The Smith Family, 2001, www.smithfamily.com.au.

Zappala Gianni, Ben Parker and Vanessa Green, *The 'New Face' of Volunteering in Social Enterprises: The Smith Family Experience*, Background Paper No. 2, Sydney: Research and Advocacy Team, The Smith Family, 2001, www.smithfamily.com.au.